What the Experts are Saying About
How to Spot Hidden Alcoholics

"An innovative and enlightening examination that eloquently describes the biology behind alcoholism, how to identify the affliction in its early stages based on behaviors, and what to do if you suspect someone you know—or don't know—has this disease. Every counselor, psychologist, physician and interventionist should read this book."

Wallace D. Winters, MD, Ph.D., Emeritus Professor
Pharmacology, Toxicology, Anesthesiology,
University of California, Davis, School of Medicine;
Retired, US FDA Medical Officer, Pacific Region

"Explaining countless tragic events that are otherwise nonsensical, Doug Thorburn makes an incontrovertible case that no dysfunction, including poverty, illiteracy and racism, causes more damage to society than alcohol and other drug addiction. A must read for every social commentator and anyone else who cares about the human condition."

Shawn Steel, former Chairperson,
California Republican Party

"Important for anyone who struggles with his own or his partner's substance abuse problem."

Glenn Sacks, men's issues columnist
and radio talk show host

"The reader will be able to uncover alcoholism before tragedies result. A remarkable book on many levels."

Thomas E. Page, LAPD, Ret.,
Drug Recognition Consultant

"Essential for anyone interested in or working in the field of alcohol and other drug addiction."

Mike Kennedy, DUI class instructor

"As an interventionist, I have seen countless families affected by a loved one's alcoholism. This gives them the tools to identify, understand and do something about the disease *before* tragedy happens."
Pat Moomey, Certified Addiction Treatment Specialist

"Doug Thorburn explains something that we all know is true: alcoholics misbehave. His observation that we can reverse this idea — misbehaviors can be an early sign of addiction, regardless of a person's social or economic status — gives us new tools that can help us *prevent* tragedy."
Joan Harter, Professor, Alcohol/Drug Studies Program, San Bernardino Valley College; President, California Association for Alcohol and Drug Educators

"Thorburn's methods can be used to help save countless lives. A must read for everyone."
Joe Pilkington, Vice President, Citizens for Truth About Alcohol Problems

"A fascinating and absorbing read from cover to cover. Doug's ideas go a long way to explain the bizarre behavior I see daily in the research for my column."
Randy Cassingham, columnist, www.ThisIsTrue.com

"My clients will benefit greatly from reading this astounding book."
Melvin Kreger, Estate and Tax Attorney

"If I had my way, I'd award a Nobel Prize to Doug Thorburn for his insightful research on how to detect a hidden alcoholic."
Irwin Zucker, Founder/President Emeritus, Book Publicists of Southern California

"You need to read this book. Most say that it doesn't apply to my friend or possible recruit. Read on — I've been there and wish I had known these ideas before."
Patricia Morrow, Executive Recruiter

How to Spot
Hidden Alcoholics

How to Spot
Hidden Alcoholics

Using Behavioral Clues to Recognize Addiction in its Early Stages

Doug Thorburn

Galt Publishing
Northridge, California

PUBLISHED BY GALT PUBLISHING
P.O. Box 7777, Northridge, CA 91327-7777

Address the author c/o Galt Publishing
or at DougThorburn@PrevenTragedy.com

Cover design by Carolyn Porter, One on One Book
Production, West Hills, California

CFP® and Certified Financial Planner® are marks owned by
the Certified Financial Planner Board of Standards, Inc.

ISBN: 0-9675788-6-8

Library of Congress Control Number: 2003114993

Printed in the United States
0 9 8 7 6 5 4 3 2 1
First Edition

Disclaimer

The purpose of this book is to educate laypersons and healthcare professionals about alcoholism. Please do not consider the information given in this
book to be the equivalent of treatment or an individual consultation. The person dealing with possible alcoholics is strongly advised to seek the help of
chemical dependency experts, as well as attend Alcoholics Anonymous and
Al-Anon meetings. This book is sold with the understanding that the author
and publisher shall have neither liability nor responsibility to any person or
entity with respect to any injury or damage caused or alleged to have been
caused, directly or indirectly, by the information in this book.

Contents

Acknowledgements

I wish to thank the addiction experts on whose shoulders I have stood, especially James Graham, Katherine Ketcham, James Milam and Vernon Johnson. In addition, Jennifer Huddleston deserves special mention as my sounding board and much-needed critic (which she will readily deny), along with Scott Dorfman who has previously offered brilliant input on communicating simply. My dear friends Mel Kreger, Joseph Sullivan and Robin Willis provided valuable advice throughout. The officers and board members of the PrevenTragedy Foundation, Pat Moomey, Patricia Morrow, Patricia Oliver Ferguson, Joan Harter, Mike Kennedy, Joe Pilkington and Robert Richards also provided moral and intellectual support. The goal of the Foundation, a tax-exempt 501c-3 organization, and of this work is to help the public better understand alcoholism and advance the idea that "early identification of alcoholism can help *prevent* tragedy." Most important, I extend my loving thanks to my favorite skeptic, my wife Marty, for having challenged me on several assumptions, without which this book could not have been written.

Introduction

One of the surprising things about alcoholism is how little most experts know. The main problem is that the definition they have agreed upon fails to describe the affliction in its early-stages. As a result, the current practice of identifying alcoholism is comparable to waiting until tumors become the size of basketballs before diagnosing cancer. Yet, almost every alcoholic shows signs of the disease years or even decades before it progresses into obvious latter-stage alcoholism. By acknowledging a difference in the processing of the drug between alcoholics and non-alcoholics, as well as between those in the early- and latter-stages of the disease, a definition can be shaped that remedies this problem. Simply put, the differential processing in the biochemistry leads to undesirable behavioral changes in those who inherit alcoholism. A definition that takes this into account allows the observer to identify the disease near its inception, increasing the odds of encouraging sobriety in the afflicted before tragedies occur.

The driving force behind the priest who molests a child, a parent who verbally or physically abuses his or her spouse and children, and the tyrant or terrorist who threatens civilization, is usually the same. This motivation is almost always egomania rooted in alcohol or other drug addiction. Journalists, biographers and historians cannot understand the compulsion that impels many of their subjects if they fail to grasp the idea of early-stage alcoholism, of which few have any knowledge.

These are bold statements. No doubt, many will wonder about my qualifications. I am not a therapist, doctor or psychiatrist. I'm not even an alcoholic. If I had been any of these, I couldn't have written this book, especially from this perspective: I would have had too much to unlearn.

Instead, I became familiar with alcoholism as a result of an intimate involvement with an alcoholic. With the goal of protecting myself in future relationships, both personal and professional, I decided to study the subject. It soon became the most fascinating topic I've ever explored. In the process, I interviewed hundreds of recovering alcoholics and read almost as many books on the subject, finally writing the most controversial book on alcoholism ever, *Drunks, Drugs & Debits: How to Recognize Addicts and Avoid Financial Abuse*. In it, I challenged the idea that alcoholics can self-diagnose and that we should all patiently wait for the inevitable "bottom." Only others can identify alcoholism in the early stages of the disease; even in the latter stages, the alcoholic must typically be coerced into sobriety. The surprising thing is that while most of this was implicit in other books on the subject, no one said it explicitly, perhaps out of fear of being seen as engaging in witch-hunts. After all, many among us have alcoholism. Yet, we are reluctant to identify alcoholics as such, because of the stigma and ingrained belief that alcoholics are bad, immoral and/or weak.

Accepting the idea that personality defects do not lead to alcoholism and that, instead, addiction causes what *appear* to be character flaws, frees us from the shame, making it far easier to diagnose the disease in others. Alcoholics are, usually, intrinsically decent people. Since they are incapable of self-diagnosis, the rest of us must learn to do so. The most effective method is to consider seemingly insignificant behavioral cues that lead to more obvious ones, even though we may never see the use of a drug. It will become evident that for every tragedy that occurs in the life of an alcoholic, there were usually dozens if not hundreds of incidents, including relatively minor misbehaviors, for which close persons and/or the law could have intervened but didn't.

We also hesitate to identify alcoholism for fear of excusing bad behaviors. Some suggest that a person afflicted through no fault of his own should not be held accountable for his or her actions. Yet, becoming clean and sober requires the imposition of responsibility and appropriate consequences. In fact, the earlier in the career of the alcoholic that private or legal sanctions are applied, the greater the chance of a return to normalcy.

This book begins by taking a look at the problems in identifying alcoholism, along with a simple explanation of its biochemistry, setting the stage for a revised definition of the disease and description of behavioral cues that inevitably follow. These are divided between early- and middle-to-latter-stage indicators and further subdivided into sets of clues within those stages. The least destructive ones, which are more numerous and less obvious as clues to alcoholism, are described in the beginning of each chapter. The more destructive indicators, generally presented towards the end of each chapter are, thankfully, rare and usually far more obvious. The general categories are divided between behaviors indicative of early-stage alcoholism in Part II and behaviors more suggestive of the middle-to-latter stages and polydrug use in Part III. Ironically, Part II behaviors tend to be other-destructive, while those in Part III are more self-destructive. The reasons for this can be found in the biochemistry, an explanation of which is therefore essential and for which I beg the reader's indulgence.

The thrust of this book is that we can — and must — identify early-stage alcohol and other drug addiction if we are to *prevent* tragedies. These include the break-up of families, domestic violence, highway slaughter, and those destructive of financial and emotional health resulting from wayward employees, co-workers, debtors and tenants. They also include the ultimate tragedy, murder, whether committed by private people or at the direction of heads of state. The drug with which we are most concerned is alcohol, because it is legal, most used and rarely suspected as the *source* of problems. However, those using other drugs, though usually more obvious, are also of concern. The drug of choice is (relatively) unimportant. Misbehaviors are indicative of the disease of addiction, which is not particular to any one drug. However, because most people think they know an "alcoholic" or two but usually not an "addict," the term "alcoholism" or "alcoholic" will generally be used to describe the overall affliction of drug addiction.

The reader should experiment with the ideas that follow. Until I began testing the hypothesis that poor conduct was usually a sign of alcoholism, I never dreamt that *a few subtle clues* might indicate a high probability of eventually proving the existence of the disease. I wouldn't expect the casual reader to blindly accept this admittedly radical idea. However, if you test the concept with people in whom you can ultimately determine are or are not alcoholics, I am confident that you will not only become convinced that this system works, but also amazed that it works so well.

This book is for lay persons and medical professionals

alike. It is meant to help the alcoholic's next victim identify him before disaster strikes, as well as to assist the medical community in identifying the source of countless other diseases and life challenges. By identifying alcoholism in the early stages, proactively imposing consequences and intervening, we significantly increase the odds of stopping the inevitable progression of the disease before an all-too-common tragic end.

PART I

Redefining Alcoholism

1

Identifying the Problem

Have you ever known someone who exhibited behaviors that didn't make sense? We always seem to figure, "That's just Billie," don't we? Or, "Suzie must have had a tough childhood," "Robbie must have a mental problem," or "Sometimes Steven acts badly in ways that are out of character with his true self. I just don't understand it; he really needs to learn to control himself."

Even experts often attribute abnormal and erratic conduct to such forces. Such was the case with James, a college student who, as part of a long-term study, was periodically interviewed by mental health professionals over several decades.

During his first interview at the age of 19, James, noted by professionals as being emotionally healthy and stable with good moral character, described his parents as warm and understanding. In a follow-up interview nine years later, shortly after his mother's death, he showed normal signs of deep grief.

At age 36, a married father of four, James went into psychiatric treatment for insomnia, guilt and anxiety. When we learn that he admitted to cheating on his wife, gambling and being deep in debt—a result of "irresponsible borrowing"— these symptoms aren't surprising. In fact, considering he had also been dismissed from his position as a university professor, it would be abnormal if he hadn't experienced deeply negative emotions.

James told therapists that his wife didn't appreciate him and that his parents, whom he had previously reported as warm, had in fact been cold. The psychiatric staff felt that his main problem was apprehension over family and job concerns, an anxiety that they believed could have originated with the death of his mother. They concluded that he had been emotionally unstable for the past 20 years, even before researchers reported that he appeared solid. *At no point did anyone consider the possibility that alcoholism might explain the behavioral changes and disorders.*

Yet, at age 50, James joined Alcoholics Anonymous. He admitted in an interview two years later that by age 30, while writing his Ph.D. thesis, he was drinking constantly and selling stolen university library books to support his drinking. He reported that he was now ashamed of what he called his "psychopathic" behavior.

The Harvard Medical School's 1990 "Mental Health Review" recited this case, originally reported by the great alcoholism authority George E. Vaillant, to illustrate "some of the problems in identifying the causes of alcoholism and making judgments about the personality of the alcoholic."[1] However, what do the causes of alcoholism have to do with this story? How are judgments about his personality relevant? The case instead illustrates that no one identified the possibility of alcoholism despite numerous behavioral indications. The message is that even medical professionals are overlooking a diagnosis of alcoholism in such cases. The "Review" didn't even identify the right problem.

On the personal side, I was romantically involved with

a beautiful and highly intelligent woman for 2 1/2 years. Like James, she exhibited increasingly bizarre behaviors and suffered from severe emotional problems. The two therapists with whom we counseled for much of that tumultuous period never once suggested the possibility that alcoholism might explain her behaviors or those of her children. Instead, they blamed me for the difficulties in our relationship, even while considering the possibility that she might have a Personality Disorder. I gradually realized that instead, she suffered from alcoholism. Surviving the experience and vowing never to go through anything like it again, I decided I'd better learn something about the subject. I happened upon Alcoholics Anonymous and realized that was a good place to start.

At AA meetings, I heard seemingly good people telling horrifying stories of atrocious behaviors in which they engaged as practicing alcoholics. This led to a very simple question: what was causing what? Did bad conduct or lack of morality cause alcoholism, or did alcoholism cause misbehaviors? As I slowly realized it was the latter, I wondered, *what if I reverse the idea?* If alcoholism caused poor behaviors, when serial misbehaviors were observed, how often might I find alcoholism? Yet, I knew from experience that alcoholics did not always act badly. Therefore, if I found a modicum of misbehaviors, might that be a harbinger of worse? These questions revolutionized my life.

Single and dating again, I began testing the idea that isolated incidents of poor conduct might be a clue to worse behaviors and, therefore, alcoholism. When I observed erratic or inexplicably destructive behaviors, I looked for evidence of addictive use. In two cases, I quickly found it and didn't stick around. One woman belittled the mutual friend who had been responsible for our introduction, a behavior that will later be shown as symptomatic of alcoholism. At the time, she was enjoying her fifth or sixth drink of the evening. Another began twisting everything I said after she popped Vicodin, which is a prescribed form of synthetic heroin, helpful for pain suppression in the non-addict and getting high for the addict. Mutual friends later confirmed my suspicions of alcohol or other drug addiction in two out of three other women, none of whom exhibited overt signs of heavy use in front of me, but who occasionally acted in uncharacteristically nasty ways. One of them drank a magnum of wine one day while working with a mutual friend and destroyed their business relationship. Another, who occasionally acted nasty, even if somewhat controlled while drinking to excess, was seen drunk several times before 10am. By considering the likely source of occasionally poor behaviors, I was able to protect myself by allowing the option of a quick exit.

More important, as the ideas developed, I began experimenting with these questions in my professional and business life. As the owner of an income tax preparation and financial planning firm, I need to hire additional employees each January. Using this tool, I began weeding out likely alcoholics. In addition, my wife and I own vacation rental town homes in Mammoth Lakes, California. I take most of the reservations and inadvertently confirmed that if I suspected alcoholism over the telephone, I was usually right. They were the guests who didn't deserve a refund from their cleaning deposit after having parties to which the police were called. I learned to inform such prospective guests that the dates they requested were unavailable.

Most important, as an Enrolled Agent (tax professional) and Certified Financial Planner licensee®, I used this idea with clients experiencing inexplicable financial problems.

If I suspected that one was romantically or professionally involved with a practicing alcoholic or other drug addict, I'd sometimes suggest the possibility. After a series of questions, I'd point to the likely culprit—even if I didn't know the person. The response was invariably something along the lines of, "No way. He's my best friend/spouse/ partner/child/parent. I've known him for twenty years. He's too smart to be an alcoholic." Countering that intelligence seems to have nothing to do with addiction, I'd suggest to my client that he* might want to take another look.

In most cases, I'd hear back a day, a month, even six months later. "You were right. How did you know?" I was confirming my theory that one can spot alcohol or other drug addiction solely on observable behaviors and their effect on others. It began to dawn on me that I was on to something with enormous ramifications.

I learned from recovering alcoholics, as well as from clients, that my story and James' are typical. The reason is that psychologists and physicians rarely receive training in this area. Therapists are usually either taught that alcoholism is caused by environmental influences, or believe this despite having learned that it's not. "You drink because your parents abused you," is a common message that many practicing alcoholics hear in therapy. In sobriety, recovering addicts tell us that the therapist was often the biggest enabler, providing all the excuses needed to

---

* Nor does gender have anything to do with addiction or codependency. Since the English language is lacking in this area, I will alternate in the use of terms signifying male or female, even though both sexes are included. For example, in almost every case, the words "he" and "she" should be thought of as "he or she."

continue drinking.** Most of the time, the therapists don't know about the drinking and, as in the case of James and my own addict, don't even suspect it. The latter may be a worse form of enabling, since they are using therapeutic techniques in a futile attempt to treat symptoms brought about by chemistry.

Until recently, medical schools required no training in the field of drug addiction. Today, they generally require at most only 24 actual classroom hours. By contrast, I have spent thousands of hours interviewing recovering alcohol and other drug addicts and researching the disease. Even psychiatrists—the drug doctors—don't get it. Dr. Martha Morrison, who tells her story in *White Rabbit: A Doctor's Story of Her Addiction and Recovery*, recounts how she was variously misdiagnosed by fellow psychiatrists as Paranoid-Schizophrenic, Obsessive-Compulsive, Bipolar, Manic, Borderline, Narcissistic, Psychotic and Sociopathic.[2] She was using almost 20 different substances a day from the age of 12 and, incredibly, went unidentified as a practicing addict until having been a licensed psychiatrist for two years. She says that she had none of these Personality Disorders and confirms that she was, quite simply, an addict. No wonder a user of the single drug alcohol, who may be only occasionally obnoxious or unreasonable, or might exhibit symptoms of what appears to be only one of these Disorders, often goes undiagnosed or, worse, misdiagnosed, for decades.

Chemical dependency experts, often referred to as "alcohol and drug abuse counselors," have the greatest

----

** We will later show that they drank addictively because their biochemistry impels them to do so. This has nothing to do with environment or one's innate psychological makeup, although these affect the form that addiction takes.

familiarity with the subject. Yet, even they sometimes lack depth of understanding. In presentations on identification of early-stage alcoholism, I ask these experts what the average age is at which one triggers alcoholism. Usually more than one member of the audience responds "age 20 or 25." I then ask, "What's the average age at which one takes his first drink in the United States?" They correctly respond, age 12 or 13. Then I say, "Let's go back to the first question." Since these experts know that the typical recovering alcoholic confides that he triggered his addiction during his first drinking episode, they quickly revise their answer.

At the beginning of these talks, I put on a bit of an act, in which I attempt to convince the audience that I will play some music on my little violin, just to get us warmed up. When I open what looks like a small violin case, I let out a shocked "oh no! I brought the wrong case!" As I reach in and pull out a bottle of what appears to be vodka, my shock turns to solace. I quickly gulp a shot and ask what this indicates. The response is, of course, alcoholism. I ask, "what stage?"

It's obviously not early-stage. For addiction to progress to the point at which the alcoholic is hiding his drug, at least one close person must have made the connection between behaviors and use. Along the way, the person I'm portraying has probably betrayed friends, ruined personal or professional relationships, and even destroyed lives. He likely has drunk beyond the legal limit and gotten behind the wheel of a car thousands of times. He has also probably displayed other misbehaviors indicative of alcoholism in private settings among friends, family and co-workers in hundreds, if not thousands, of incidents. Yet the odds are that only a few have ever suggested that he "drinks too much," almost no one has explained that the use is responsible for the bad behaviors, and he's never been the subject of a professionally aided intervention.

Few, "experts" included, are identifying alcoholism until it becomes tragically obvious. There are a number of reasons for this potentially lethal delay in diagnosis. The main one is that the commonly accepted definition of alcoholism, approved by the National Council on Alcoholism and Drug Dependence (NCADD) and the American Society of Addiction Medicine (ASAM), precludes the possibility of early identification. Yet, in the next chapter, we will show that the flaw in the definition should be obvious from the biochemistry.

2

A Matter of Biochemistry

We can all spot the latter-stage drunk. The person who's already lost his job, family and all sense of self-worth has also eliminated something else: the brain's ability to produce "feel-good" neurotransmitters, such as endorphins and dopamine (see Appendix II), in sufficient quantities to feel right on its own. He needs the substance to "normalize." This takes many years of heavy use, usually at least three decades (and often far longer), if he uses only the drug alcohol.

As I heard the stories of recovering alcoholics in AA, I began asking myself how they got to the point at which they lost control over their use. In my college fraternity, many of us did our best to "become" alcoholics. Most couldn't, although later the affliction became obvious in a few. In college, these were the ones who could drink the rest of us under the table—but at the time, I didn't know it. I wasn't counting the drinks and they didn't appear inebriated with blood alcohol levels at which others could barely walk. What was different about these men, whose alcoholism later became obvious? What allowed them to drink so much that they eventually diminished their own brain's ability to produce neurotransmitters? I realized that the only thing that could explain this was that the body of the alcoholic had to be processing the drug differently than the non-alcoholic. I began to suspect that latter stage alcoholism might result from a difference in early-stage biochemistry, with which we are born.

It turns out that the early-stage biology of a person who develops alcoholism does not just allow him to drink excessively; it *motivates* him to do so. With enough heavy use, he eventually reaches the point at which his neurotransmitter activity suffers. The early-stage biochemistry of the person who inherits alcoholism also causes specific brain damage that results in destructive behaviors. The distinction between early-stage alcoholics and non-alcoholics is in a differential processing that involves two chemicals, acetaldehyde and acetate.

The human body converts alcohol into acetaldehyde, a poison, and then into acetate. However, the speed with which the conversion occurs varies. Non-alcoholics make the transformation slowly into acetaldehyde and very quickly into acetate, resulting in a buildup of the latter substance. This provides the equivalent of immunity from alcoholism because, while otherwise harmless, acetate causes feelings of nausea, hangover and sleepiness. These are felt at relatively low blood alcohol levels in the non-alcoholic, in most cases .06 to .10 per cent (barely legally drunk).

The person with alcoholism, on the other hand, converts alcohol into acetaldehyde quickly and then into acetate very slowly. The resulting increase in levels of acetaldehyde causes a release of neurotransmitters called isoquinolines, opiate-like substances that make him feel really good.[3] Therefore, there's no feedback from a buildup of acetate suggesting "slow it down" as there is in the non-alcoholic. Instead, a voice soaked in acetaldehyde says, "keep on truckin', you're feeling fine!" At the same time, the chemical causes brain poisoning, resulting in brain damage.

This damage is particular to the neo-cortex of the brain, the seat of reason and logic. Because the lower brain center, the limbic system, is fixed at birth, it escapes the deluge of chemistry relatively unscathed. Referred to as the pre-mammalian or "reptilian" brain, the limbic system is the origin of basic instincts, including impulsive actions and reactions responsible for survival and procreation. Damage to the "human" part of the brain leaves the primitive area in relatively greater control over behaviors. This may explain the tendency to act without considering consequences, along with the manifestation of other uncivilized behaviors. Because few non-alcoholics exhibit such conduct, we can predict that most persons convicted of felonies would be afflicted with this disease. *The fact that at least 80-90% of incarcerated prisoners have alcoholism supports these ideas.*[4]

Damage to the neo-cortex also leads to a decline in the ability to accurately perceive and judge, resulting in distortions of perceptions and memory. The key distortion is one that is apparent in all persons with alcoholism: euphoric recall.[5] This causes the addict to remember ("recall") that everything he says or does during a drinking episode is good or right, and nothing bad or wrong. Since only God is always good or right, this might be predicted to result in behaviors that make the addict appear to think he is god-like. We will find that the observable evidence in the form of behaviors not only bear this out, but also that such behaviors provide our best and most numerous clues to early-stage alcoholism. They are common because they occur both during and in-between drinking episodes.

This sense of god-likeness leads the alcoholic to develop an inordinately large sense of self-importance, or "inflated ego." We find that almost every alcoholic in the early stages of his disease exhibits this and has an observable need to further inflate that ego. He does so in three all-encompassing ways:

1. wielding power over others, especially capriciously;
2. acting recklessly, as if to say "watch what I can do/get away with"; and
3. over-achievement.

The last explains what may be the grand paradox of alcoholism: the early-stage, highly tolerant "functional" alcoholic, who may even be an extraordinary success. This is often the alcoholic with the greatest potential for becoming lethal or otherwise harmful to others. He is rarely diagnosed and, therefore, usually goes untreated. He is frequently not only excused for his behaviors, but also protected from consequences by family, friends, fans, constituents and even law enforcers. The path of destruction can, therefore, carry on for decades. The question we need to ask is, why are we waiting? Why do we so often allow tragedy to occur before counteracting alcoholism?

3

Alcoholism Redefined

We wait in part because, as the great linguist S.I. Hayakawa explained, thoughts and beliefs are often determined by the words we use and their definitions.[6] For example, the words "he's an alcoholic" sound like an accusation. A person is called this with about the same reverence as being identified as a leper. The implication is that lack of willpower, character, or morality causes alcoholism. The reaction is often "Why not give him the benefit of the doubt and *not* assume alcoholism?" Since the biochemistry has never before been explained simply, few truly understand that cause and effect are opposite. Believing that character weaknesses cause alcoholism makes it difficult to diagnose the disease. The retort should be, "I *am* giving him the benefit, because if he doesn't have alcoholism, he's probably a truly bad person. On the other hand, if he has alcoholism, there is hope for him."

Most important, the commonly accepted definition of alcoholism is not consistent with early-stage biochemistry and instead describes mostly latter-stage symptoms. *While the experts agree that about 10% of the U.S. population have alcoholism, the definition allows for its identification in far fewer than one out of ten.* And, it does little to shed light on behaviors.

This is the definition that the most important national organizations in the field of alcoholism and medical professionals practicing addiction medicine jointly agreed to in 1990:

> "Alcoholism/Chemical Dependency is a primary, chronic disease with genetic, psychosocial and environmental factors influencing its development and manifestation. The disease is often progressive and fatal, and is characterized by continuous or periodic:
> 1. impaired control over drinking/using,
> 2. preoccupation with the drug,
> 3. use of alcohol/drug despite adverse consequences and
> 4. distortion in thinking, most notably denial."

Because this definition is in such wide use and has such great acceptance by the professionals, its meaning filters down to lay persons. Unfortunately, it is useless in attempting to diagnose early-stage alcoholics. We can see why by analyzing it piece by piece.

• "Alcoholism/Chemical Dependency" – the term "dependency" suggests a physical dependence on the substance, which as seen in the biochemistry may not occur for decades.

• "primary, chronic disease" – This is correct. "Primary" means that it is the cause of other conditions and is not caused by any other disorder. The primary disease must be cleared up before secondary problems can be successfully treated. It's chronic because, absent treatment, it continues unabated. It's a disease not in the sense of germs or viruses, but rather like diabetes: there is an abnormal processing of an ingested chemical.

• "with genetic, psychosocial and environmental factors influencing its development and manifestation." — Correct, but with a caveat. It is genetic; some children get it, some don't. It skips around generations, as do many diseases. The virulence of addiction inherited, the psychology of the person[7] and the environment, all influence the form addiction takes. The definition is flawed, however, in failing to point out that its inception is essentially 100% predetermined in a person who possesses the necessary alcoholic biochemistry and begins using the drug. By neglecting to include the idea that psychological, social and environmental factors cannot change biochemistry, there is an implication that a person with alcoholism, if properly treated, can safely resume use. Numerous studies purporting to show this have failed when taking into account long-term control over behaviors.

• "The disease is often progressive and fatal" — Agreed. Unfortunately, this does not point to the most gruesome reality of alcoholism: that it is extremely damaging and sometimes fatal *to others* often before the afflicted succumbs.

• "characterized by continuous or periodic:" — The periodic heavy drinker is the most difficult to identify as alcoholic, especially in the early stage, when months or even years may elapse between uses. Therefore, the observer is at a disadvantage in making a prognosis of a periodic vs. continuous user. *Note that the four criterion that follow include an "and" between items three and four, not an "or." This suggests that all four are necessary for a diagnosis of alcoholism.*

• "impaired control over drinking/using" — This is key. How did the person with alcoholism get to the point at which he has lost such control? As previously stated, it can take decades of heavy use for the biochemistry to change. *This loss of control occurs only in latter stage alcoholism.* Those in the early stage often go for weeks, months or years either without drinking, or controlling their use. The poly-drug addict often loses control early on, but this makes him easier to diagnose and may push him into latter-stage addiction at a chronologically young age. Furthermore, most outsiders (and often, even close persons) are not in a position to observe loss of control over use: it is too often hidden.

• "preoccupation with the drug" — Until he needs the drug to normalize, why would there be an obsession? Because he knows how incredibly good and righteous it makes him feel. However, only he knows this; the *feeling* of godliness that occurs in the early stage is not observable by another person. It is unlikely that others will see behaviors indicating obsession until the latter stage, when a continuous flow of the drug can be found coursing through his veins.

• "use of alcohol/drug despite adverse consequences" — The expression "alcohol/drug" suggests that alcohol is not a drug. The terminology would be greatly improved by saying, "alcohol/other drug," which makes it clear that alcohol is a subcategory. "Adverse consequences" are: 1) in the eye of the beholder; 2) often not suffered in the early stage because (a) the alcoholic is protected from consequences by well-meaning friends, family, fans, constituents and even law enforcers and (b) over-achievement often compensates for negative consequences; 3) rarely connected to use by the afflicted because of euphoric recall (viewing everything he says or does in a self-favoring light). Therefore, "adverse consequences" is not a terribly useful indicator of alcoholism, especially in the early stage.

• "and" — The use of the word "and" is troubling, since if any of these criteria are met, alcoholism usually exists. Furthermore, since few observers are privy to any of the criteria, such guidelines are often useless in diagnosing addiction at *any* stage until the addict's life has completely fallen apart.

• "distortion in thinking, most notably denial" — Alcoholism causes distortions in perception and memory, which inevitably lead to impaired thinking and judgment. The most notable distortion is euphoric recall. Since this makes the person with early-stage alcoholism believe that he can do no wrong or that his drug and biochemistry cannot be the source of problems in his life or in the lives of those around him, he cannot be in denial. Denial implies a willful attempt to not admit to something. Since alcoholism causes self-favoring distortions of perception and memory, there is nothing left to admit. One cannot be in denial about something that he is incapable of seeing.

This description provides little help in identifying the person with early-stage alcoholism. The key flawed criterion is loss of control over use, which occurs only as a result of latter-stage biochemistry or by using a drug far more physically addictive than alcohol. While such drugs are laser-like in the targeting of neurotransmitters, alcohol takes a "shot-gun" approach. This allows the latter to affect practically all of the neurotransmitters, albeit to a relatively weak degree, thereby slowing the speed with which one can become physically addicted. This accounts for the fact that it can take decades before withdrawal from alcohol becomes excruciatingly painful or deadly.[8]

Furthermore, adverse consequences are frequently not experienced at all in the early stage. The outsider cannot observe the depth to which there is a preoccupation, even if some of the outward effects can be seen. However, the constant craving for the drug as represented in movies such as "Lost Weekend" simply does not occur in this stage. The definition completely misses the descriptor that the early-stage biochemistry predicts: loss of control over behaviors and, in particular, destructive conduct. Since these occur near the onset, the behavioral manifestations of addiction need to be included in the definition. The following takes this into account:

> *Alcoholism is a genetic disorder that causes the afflicted to biochemically process the drug alcohol in such a way as to cause that person to engage in destructive behaviors, at least some of the time.*

This definition suggests that the biochemistry that causes a genetic predisposition in the afflicted, differs from that of the non-afflicted. It provides a set of observable symptoms ("destructive behaviors") that are often evident only erratically ("at least some of the time"). This makes it possible to identify those with alcoholism long before obvious latter-stage symptoms appear, affording the opportunity for close persons, as well as others acting under the protection or guise of law, to intervene and *prevent* tragedy, rather than react to it.

Once we know what to look for, early-stage signs and symptoms are obvious long before we actually see excessive drinking. The indicators rest upon the quintessential fact that the alcoholic's distorted perceptions inevitably result in impaired judgment, which always emerge in misbehaviors. *The best and earliest clues to addiction, then, are behavioral.*

The behaviors can be categorized as indicative more of early-stage, middle-stage/polydrug, or latter-stage alcoholism. By the time the afflicted is in the latter stage, he has likely been identified as having the disease and multiple tragedies have occurred, or are in the process of unfolding. Therefore, this stage will not be our focus. Another system of categories will overlay the subdivision by early and middle stage addiction:

1. "Supreme being" complex
2. Signs of a sense of invincibility
3. Evidence of repeated poor judgment
4. Apparent mental confusion
5. Physical signs.

Here also, the behaviors are largely a result of one or the other of these, with some having multiple sources. The first two sets, "supreme being" and invincibility, are driven by the alcoholic's need to inflate his ego and are found under early-stage signs. Poor judgment and mental confusion are generally symptomatic of middle-stage addiction and beyond, at which point the destructive behaviors toward others more often result from alcoholism-induced errors or a desire to obtain the drug regardless of cost than from attempts at inflating the ego. Some of these also suggest latter-stage alcoholism, when the person becomes far more self-destructive than other-destructive. While physical signs fall into early, middle and latter stages, don't let the categories limit your ability to diagnose: they are not set in stone, many of the symptoms cross boundaries, and there are plenty of instances where early-stage behavioral clues are found with middle-stage physical signs. Sometimes, extended use causes the body to begin to give out long before the mind.

PART II

Early-Stage Clues

-

"When I have one martini, I feel bigger, wiser, taller. When I have a second, I feel superlative. When I have more, there's no holding me."
William Faulkner[9]

4

A "Supreme Being" Complex

Addiction expert Harry M. Tiebout, MD in his 1954 article, "The Ego Factors in Surrender to Alcoholism," was among the first to explain the inordinately large sense of self-importance observable in alcoholics. He distinguished what he called an "inflated ego" from Sigmund Freud's ego (a personality aspect between id and superego), yet integrated this inflated self-view with Freud's observations regarding infants. Tiebout pointed out that the alcoholic ego emanates from three infantile factors. The relevant one for our purpose is the infant's psyche, summarized in Freud's brilliant summation, "His Majesty, the Baby." The infant "is born ruler of all he surveys."[10] This suggests an omnipotence proffering special rights, privileges and positions, as if godlike.

1. Over-achiever, due to a need to win at any cost

Half way through writing *Drunks, Drugs & Debts*,[11] I realized I was examining behaviors that I didn't completely understand. By this time, I knew that the root cause of most destructive behaviors, society's woes and human dysfunctions was substance addiction. However, I was unable to reconcile alcoholism with extraordinary accomplishments. I couldn't make sense of the puzzle probably best exemplified by the baseball great, Ty Cobb.

Coincidentally, at this time I met a great grand niece of Cobb's. When I told her about this seemingly inexplicable riddle, she suggested that we view her copy of the "Ty Cobb Story" together. Arguably the greatest baseball player who ever lived, with a lifetime batting average of over .400, Cobb clearly had full-blown alcoholism during his entire career. He did everything possible to destroy those closest to him. We saw him sharpen his cleats so that when he stole a base he would have the opportunity to seriously harm the person he slid into. He was portrayed as a monster, yet his grand niece told me that the stories she had heard about his exploits were far worse. How could this conduct, driven by alcoholism, be reconciled with extraordinary success?

A week later the answer came as I began reading James Graham's explanation of the ego factors in alcoholism. Forty years after Tiebout's article was published, Graham wrote that alcoholism causes egomania and that competency and high performance, whether in a legal or illegal business, profession or act, are ways by which to inflate that ego. Successful ego inflation, in turn, seems to feed early-stage alcoholism, further fueling the ego.[12] Egomania in any form appears to halt the otherwise inevitable progression of the disease, allowing the alcoholic to remain in the early stages — and hence, identified as such by few, if any — far longer than those less capable.

This would account for what Graham refers to as the "superb specimens," those whom we would never otherwise suspect as having this disease. Many thousands of top entertainers and professional athletes have had alcoholism. In her study of well-known female alcoholics, Lucy Barry Robe estimated that 30% of Academy Award® winning actors were afflicted, far in excess of the percentage of alcoholics in the U.S. population.[13] Donald Goodwin, MD, found that 30% of famous American writers also had alcoholism, including five out of the seven Nobel Prize-winning authors from the United States during the 20th Century.[14] Alcoholics are believed to comprise a higher percentage of extremely successful lawyers, CEOs of major corporations and politicians than the overall population.

Katherine Ketcham and James Milam point out that performance can improve in early-stage addiction.[15] Graham theorizes that ambition increases due to egomania resulting from alcoholism. Now combine these ideas: an exploding ambition with an increasingly inflated ego drives performance in early-stage alcoholism, which may be a significant clue to this disease near its inception.

Over-achievement does not mean that one is an alcoholic. However, it could be argued that not only does such success allow for it, but also that its existence may be slightly higher for over-achievers. The need to satiate the ego can, in the early stages, drive competencies. Therefore, rather than overlooking the possibility of alcoholism due to accomplishments, we might instead double up our efforts in identifying it. This is requisite if the achievements are the result of a need to win regardless of cost (i.e., at the expense of others) and there are any other signs evident. In the case of the overachieving alcoholic, the observer must be particularly mindful of the late alcoholism expert James E. Royce's adage that we don't find alcoholism unless we look for it.[16]

Nor should we ignore the possibility of alcoholism in top athletes, entertainers, business and/or political leaders just because the lives of well-known personalities are so public. On the contrary, recovering alcoholic and ex-wife of Michigan's former Lt. Gov. James Brickley, Marianne E. Brickley, observed that the higher an addict's social status, the greater the enabling.[17] This is due to the fact that because of the potential for disgrace, their enablers have so much to lose. "Business," "professional," "political" and "military" can be added to "social." In business, due to the stigma of alcoholism, enablers have their jobs and incomes at stake if their boss's secret is uncovered. In the entertainment industry, not only are jobs and incomes at risk, but also fame and prestige. We can add "power" to the myriad of benefits that enablers of those in high political office stand to relinquish. This is the reason that employees lie for the addict, ignore their drunken incidents or behavior, cover up and obtain their drugs for them, even violating the law themselves to protect the secret. Therefore, we are less likely to know that a person holding high office in public or private employment has the disease of alcoholism.

2. Regularly uses foul language

Such language is not the sole province of alcoholics, but it is common among them. It is also prevalent among codependents, who learn—but may unlearn—this manner of inflating the ego. Screenplay writers often get it right, portraying those swearing as heavy drinkers or other drug users. In real life we usually find that a person who curses with regularity exhibits additional confirming signs of alcoholism. This relatively innocuous behavior is, in civilized cultures, a method of suggesting that one is more important than are others, especially when used to demean.

3. Smokes cigarettes

Despite legal proscriptions, smoking usually begins in the teen years. The "look at me, I'm cool" attitude helps to trigger the habit which, as we all know, soon turns addictive. However, tobacco is not a psychoactive drug. By itself, it does not cause distortions in perception, even if it causes a craving that few can overcome without great difficulty. Therefore, the behavior patterns of smokers who are not alcoholics are generally no more destructive than those of other non-addicts.

On the other hand, smoking can be an important clue to alcoholism. For an as-yet-undetermined reason, 90% of all alcoholics are heavy cigarette smokers.[18] About 25% of Americans smoke. Alcoholics comprise about 10% of the U.S. population. If 90% of these are smokers, we can conclude that more than one third (by calculation, 9/25ths) have alcoholism. Therefore, someone observed smoking in the U.S. has more than three times the odds of having alcoholism as does a non-smoker.

This information can be used to weed out likely alcoholics in a variety of situations that may be helpful to one's financial and emotional health. I point out to prospective vacation-home rental guests who I suspect may have addiction that smoking is not allowed on the premises. When the response is, "Oh, don't worry, we only smoke outside," the prospect is steered elsewhere. When an inordinately large sense of self-importance is on display, we should be on guard. If the person is a smoker, the odds of alcoholism are significantly increased.

On the road, this can prove to be life saving. If the window is down on a really hot or cold day, we don't even need to see him smoking to greatly increase the odds of alcoholism and, therefore, a possible DUI: he may be airing out the car. Drug Recognition Experts, police officers who are highly skilled in the detection of alcohol and other drugs, have told me that just seeing a window down on such days causes them to look twice at the driver. If that's the first thing you see, watch the behaviors. If he begins weaving in and out of traffic and tailgating, as if to say "get out my way! I'm more important than you and deserve to be in front," do what he suggests and get out of his way.

4. Extraordinarily charming

The most magnificent portrayal ever of an alcoholic on the big screen is probably Al Pacino's characterization of Lt. Col. Frank Slade in "Scent of a Woman." Slade was blinded when, after having four vodka screwdrivers for breakfast, he juggled hand grenades. Displaying reckless behavior and a grand sense of invincibility, he pulled the pin out of one. It exploded in his face and destroyed his vision.

The story takes place one Thanksgiving weekend, when his caregivers (niece and family) decide to go away. They hire a sitter, Charlie Sims. As soon as the family is gone, Slade takes Sims on a hedonistic journey to New York City, where he intends to live it up for one last weekend before committing suicide. Having a dinner he can ill-afford at the Waldorf, his other powerful senses detect a young lady of Sims' age. Playing matchmaker, Slade exhibits a charm so bedazzling and exciting that the viewer may develop chills watching him sweep the young lady onto the dance floor, teaching her the Tango even though blind. The process of inflating the ego is so multi-faceted that it mocks the prevalent views of alcoholism.

A common belief among therapists is that non-alcoholics who fall in love with alcoholics are sick. Yet, when we consider how talented and charming the alcoholic can be, it's surprising that this does not occur more often. In addition, the non-alcoholic child of an addict is accustomed to the erratic behaviors. These considerations, along with the fact that conservative personality types are often attracted to their opposites — reckless styles driven even more so by alcoholism — account for the excess of betrothals to the afflicted by non-alcoholics.

5. Occupational choices that allow the wielding of power or ease of use

The question of why so many extraordinarily successful actors and athletes have alcoholism is a vexing one. These are people who, by the nature of their trade, must keep fit. Actors generally take the lead in healthful diet fads and often go to extremes to keep their faces wrinkle-free. In the long run, alcoholism damages the heart, liver and other organs; it more quickly ages the face and the rest of the body as well. Eventually, it reduces the strength required of professional athletes. What could account, then, for the incidence of a large percentage of addicts in these and certain other occupations?

Recall that alcoholism is often triggered in the teen years, usually around age 13. It acts quickly to cause an inordinately large sense of self-importance, requiring that the afflicted person further inflate his ego. The question raised in adolescence is, even if subconsciously, in what profession can the ego be inflated most effectively?

Certain occupations more easily allow participants to

wield power than do others. Power can take many forms. Power over one's audience is attractive to the fledgling entertainer, whether actor, musician or athlete. Street thugs wield capricious power over innocent people. Law enforcers can, to a degree, determine which criminals will experience the wrath of their powers, while politicians decide which constituents will benefit from the use of theirs. Subconsciously or not, the addict chooses his profession in part based on the degree to which he can control others. The more arbitrary, erratic and whimsical, the greater the power.

Many have observed the high incidence of alcoholism not only among well-known celebrities, but also among war heroes and police officers, attributed to the "stresses and strains" of being such. If life's stresses caused alcoholism, we would all be alcoholics. Instead, alcoholism precedes the courageous behavior and, in fact, contributes to it based on the need to boost the ego. This thesis is supported by a U.S. Navy study that found an astonishing 46% of recruits with "an identifiable history of problem drinking" at the time of enlistment.[19] It is also supported anecdotally. The lowball estimate of the percentage of active-duty police officers with alcoholism on any force from which Drug Recognition Officers were interviewed for this and prior books was 20%, and as high as 50% in some smaller police departments. The estimates that dozens of recovering ex-cons, former guards and chemical dependency experts provided on the percentage of prison guards who have alcoholism range from a frightening 50% to a horrifying 80%. For some, there is no more effective way to inflate one's ego than by wielding power over prisoners, for whom fighting back is not a viable option.

Professions that offer easy access to drugs may attract

more addicts as well. Medical doctors, especially psychiatrists and pharmacists, have reportedly high incidences of
substance addiction. Bear in mind that it's difficult to
obtain reliable statistics about the prevalence of a disease
that nobody thinks they have until they are in recovery.
For obvious reasons, this is compounded when identifying
rates of addiction among such professionals. Because of the
fact that the stigma of alcoholism is too great to give published statistics any degree of accuracy and that addicts are
often supremely competent at work, few with early-stage
alcoholism are identified. Doctors in recovery have reported that they have performed entire surgeries during blackouts, much in the same way that alcoholic pilots have
flown Boeing 747s, "coming to" in mid-air, wondering
where they were heading. Ease of access to drugs is also
found in occupations with flexible schedules, such as sales.
When they drink heavily, they can do so inconspicuously.
The ease of use and flexibility in work allows many in the
contracting trades to use excessively on the job as well,
accounting for what may be an extraordinarily high percentage of alcohol and other drug addicts among trades-
men.[20]

6. Engages in risky behaviors in reckless fashion

While many alcoholics rarely engage in risky behaviors, some do so regularly. It usually begins in early-stage
alcoholism for those predisposed to such conduct. A sense
of invincibility may explain unnecessarily risky behaviors,
while later in the progression of the disease, impaired
judgment may better explain many of these actions.

However, the sense of godliness and the idea that one
is the Supreme Being naturally leads one to engage in risky
acts. Many with extraordinary athletic prowess are driven

by their alcoholism. Numerous captains of industry, many of whom acted recklessly to mankind's benefit, have had this disease. The fact that early-stage alcoholism drives achievement and can actually improve performance, in turn reinforcing the idea that one is on par with God, accounts for much of this risk-taking.

Unnecessary risks are those that provide the most obvious evidence of alcoholism. Henri Paul took such risks. Princess Diana paid for his behaviors with her life.

7. Has a "the rules don't apply to me" attitude

The most special of rights and privileges is to be an exception under the law. If the exception is legal, that is good. No doubt, alcoholics are the best lobbyists when it comes to obtaining such special privileges. But if not within the law, so much the better if they get away with it. There is little else that increases the size of the ego more effectively than flouting legal prohibitions.

Alcoholism's main distortion, euphoric recall, leads the addict to truly think that he can do no wrong. If he violates the rules, it is the rule, not he, that is wrong.

The observable evidence for the idea that many persons with addiction act in this way can be found inside any prison. There is also evidence in the case of lesser crimes. One instance was that of a Floridian whose vanity license plate "JST CRZY" was photographed 705 times in a 10-month period zipping through tollbooths without paying. After finally being stopped and facing a $15,000 fine, he was reported to have responded, "I'm such a good person. People who know me just can't believe this is happening." He explained that someone must have stole his license plate and put it on a car similar to his own. However, he couldn't explain his dozen convictions for speeding and drunk driving.[21]

These rule-breakers can be found in many homes and inside every school. While some children are naturally rebellious, the attitude becomes more defiant when alcoholism is triggered. Those children who do not develop alcoholism, grow up and largely dispense with the more excessive anti-social behaviors. However, alcoholics do not mature emotionally, and account for most insubordinate behavior in the workplace. While sedition can be a good thing, greater harm than good often results when an alcoholic leads the insurgence.

8. Compulsive gambler

Recall that the alcoholic suffers brain damage to the neo-cortex, which allows the pre-mammalian limbic system to run amuck. Impulses are not reigned in and compulsive behaviors often result.

Some are compulsive without the aid of a drug. However, these types of people are even quicker to act on impulse while they are practicing addicts. Recovering alcoholics occasionally disagree with me, suggesting that they are as bad now as they were when using. Two responses are appropriate: one, due to euphoric recall, they don't remember how awful their behaviors were before their recovery, even if they later (well into sobriety) figure it out based on the repercussions of their actions. Two, they often flip into other compulsions in early abstinence. Terence Gorski, a relapse prevention specialist, provides evidence that many such addicts substitute or continue in these behaviors, including gambling.[22] They may do so in an attempt to boost their crumbling ego.

Recovery requires the cessation of drug use (including drinking) and, at the same time, ego deflation. Stopping the drinking does not by itself deflate the ego, which accounts for millions of "dry drunks." These alcoholics are not in recovery and are, therefore, between drinking episodes. They are capable of engaging in behaviors every bit as destructive as practicing alcoholics even if they often don't.

The behaviors include compulsive gambling, spending and sex. According to recovering alcoholic-gambler Mike Brubaker, the percentage of gamblers who are active or "recovering" substance addicts is about 50%.[23] If in recovery from alcoholism, substitution of one compulsive behavior for another complicates and interferes with recovery. Gorski suggests that such behaviors allow the process of relapse to begin.[24] Hence, substitutions of compulsions clue us in to the fact that the addict is not in good, solid recovery and that a relapse may occur at any time.

9. Compulsive spender

I once had a conversation with a client who is good friends with an extremely well known entertainer who, I was told, was in recovery from substance addiction. When I asked my client if I could meet with the entertainer to discuss my work, he said he would see whether an introduction could be arranged. I then asked how long she had been in recovery. His response was, "She stopped her cocaine and heroin use about five years ago."

It took me a couple of minutes to grasp the significance of his words, at which point I asked how long she had been in recovery from *alcoholism*. His response shocked me: "Oh, she still drinks." I told him in that case, she wasn't in recovery since, to an addict, alcohol is just like any other psychotropic drug in its ability to cause distortions of perception and memory.

He didn't understand this. He said she was so much better now that she had stopped using illegal drugs. She was no longer late for every appointment, didn't lie the way she did before and wasn't physically deteriorating as quickly. I told him that since she was an alcoholic (as almost all other-drug addicts are), there had to be some method by which she continued to inflate her ego. I suggested that she might be doing this in a fairly big way. After several more minutes of discussion, it finally hit him: she spent money in ways the rest of us can only dream.

He told me of hundred thousand dollar shopping sprees in which multi-thousand dollar gowns were purchased that she'd wear only once, if ever. There were stories of picking up the food and drink tabs for complete strangers in an entire restaurant. She inflated her ego by saying, "Look at what I can afford," even while she went deeper in debt. Every once in a while we read about seemingly wealthy entertainers who, it turns out, have more debt than assets and eventually declare bankruptcy. This may seem surprising, yet it's so easy with alcoholism. And if their ego manifesting in overspending doesn't do them in, eventually impaired judgment resulting in money mismanagement will.

This is a compulsion that can exist independently of alcoholism, but rarely is it totally isolated. Many instances of compulsive spending take root in the codependent child who experienced a sense of psychological abandonment as the parent carried on a love affair with the drug. The child attempts to make up for this loss, in gambling, sexual escapades and/or by purchasing extravagant goods and services in a futile attempt to replace the parent they cherished, who was incapable of returning that love.

10. Pontificates

To pontificate is to be dogmatic, to assert without proof and in an arrogant manner. The more pompous sounding, the greater the likelihood of alcoholism. After all, pompous, "having or exhibiting marked self-importance," is close to our definition of inflated ego, "an inordinately large sense of self-importance." It's a question of degree. There may also be a measure of bombast, defined as "high-sounding language without meaning".

11. Uses twisted logic to get his or her way or to win the argument

Alcoholics are able to twist and turn logic upside down. Some do this in personal or professional relationships. For example, a bill for services performed was presented to a client. Prior to payment, additional services were requested and provided. Another bill was sent and, after several months, a letter was received stating, "It is my belief that you have already been compensated through a pre-arranged contract with my parents." Later in the note he says, "at no point did I agree to compensate you for this work."

In another instance, a tax professional's client was under audit for a possible large underreporting of income. The client became belligerent while preparing the current year return, insisting on taking a deduction for a home mortgage he had helped pay, but for which he was not obligated (his girlfriend owned the home). He later asked, "What would my taxes be if I was getting the interest deduction I deserve from our home mortgage? Why aren't you finding a way for me to take that deduction?" Then, after stopping payment on a check for the completed return, he wrote, "I noted a substantial error in the return.

My interest deduction was omitted for whatever reason. If you will correct the return, I'll send you another check." Yeah, right.

Addicts engage in doublethink, in which wrong is right and right is wrong. The addict is not rude, you are. He is not insane, you are. He doesn't lie; you do, etc. Psychological gamesmanship results from a need to control others in unpredictable fashion, thereby keeping those around him off-center, always guessing. If you never know what's coming next, you become far less capable of protecting yourself. This confers tremendous power in the alcoholic.

This may take form in intellectuals as mind-games. To insure that they are seen as more intelligent than you, such games may lead to twisted and contorted threads of logic that only they can follow. Sometimes, for good reason: when carefully analyzed, they make no sense.

12. Is a great liar

There are three main reasons that account for the fact that alcoholics are the world's most persuasive liars. One is that there is no sneakier way by which to wield control over others than by lying.

There are several main ways in which the addict controls others through lies. The most destructive, perhaps, is the making of false accusations, discussed under its own heading. Twisted logic and charm involve other variations of lying. Serial Don Juanism, especially taking form in serial adultery requires lying or deceit. Sometimes alcoholics lie just to prove what they can get away with. Some show this by acting recklessly on the road; others do so with reckless abandon abusing people's minds.

The great liars of the world include con artists. It is not

so much the taking of money that excites them as it is the game of seeing whom they can con; although, the money provides power as well. Many of the great con men throughout history may have been alcoholics. However, there are large gaps in the histories of these men, because their biographers never knew that heavy use of alcohol was relevant to understanding them.

One of the greatest con men ever was Charles Ponzi, from whom the term "Ponzi scheme" is derived. The idea behind this scam, which continues today in varied forms, is to promise exceptionally high returns on one's investment. The trouble is that new funds are not invested; they are instead used to pay previous investors the fantastic returns promised. Obviously, the scam is uncovered sooner or later, when it collapses because of a dearth of new investors.

Ponzi's biographer Donald H. Dunn mentions Ponzi's drinking only a few times over a span of 254 pages. At one point, he tells of Ponzi drinking white wine "quickly in several gulps" and of needing pills for the sour stomach because he had "too much wine today."[25] That he drank despite the fact that he carried the pills for "sour stomach" with him is indicative of alcoholism. He added a "heavy splash of anisette to his fourth cup of coffee," and ended the day with "a large meal and innumerable glasses of fine French wine." Dunn tells us at the outset that the events recorded were as factually true as his extensive research could make them, and that "although treated novelistically, *what* happens is grounded thoroughly in reality."[26] Long after his scheme collapsed, divorced, out of prison and deported to Italy in the mid-1930s, he was given enough cash by high-ranking friends "for the aging swindler to get drunk frequently and gamble...in a neighborhood bar."[27] This was the extent that Dunn remarked on Ponzi's drinking. Considering the fact that he had no idea it was even relevant and that the events were grounded in reality, the likelihood of alcoholism being the motive force behind his need to swindle others is high.

Another reason why addicts become great liars is to protect either their source of drugs, which is common among illegal drug addicts, or the fact that they are using at all, routine with latter-stage alcoholics.

The third reason is that the addict may, quite simply, not remember the truth. This occurs most often in convincing fashion due to euphoric recall, remembering everything in a self-favoring light. Along with blackouts and memory repression, this gives an *appearance* of lying. As observers, we may be unable to distinguish between the basis for the lies. As the lying proliferates, regardless of reason, the odds of addiction increase.

The warning labels of various psychotropic drugs prescribed by doctors include impaired speech and memory, paranoia, drowsiness and mental confusion. Labels on alcohol warn that consumption impairs the ability to drive a car or operate machinery, that drinking may cause problems and that women should not drink during pregnancy because of the risk of birth defects. These warnings in a more enlightened society might include an increased probability of lying and the commission of other destructive behaviors directed at others.

13. Repeatedly makes promises that are not kept

This is a variation of lying, but is mentioned separately because the excuses alcoholics drum up are meant to convince close persons that failing to keep promises can be justified, or that promises were actually never made. For example, there may be parsing about the meaning of the word "will," as in "I will do this or that." To suggest that the typical alcoholic is manipulative is to seriously understate the point. This is one of those tactics designed to keep everyone around him unbalanced.

14. Belittles others

Alcoholics inflate their egos at the expense of others. A relatively innocuous way to do this is by making disparaging and belittling remarks of another. Such behaviors can be a subtle clue to alcoholism, or to an impending relapse. I once watched a person who was a known recovering alcoholic make such comments to his girlfriend for the better part of an hour. He'd alternate his putdowns with just enough charm and niceties to keep her off guard, compelling her to sit through repeated rounds of verbal abuse.

I spoke with him a few days later and told him that he had either relapsed, or was subconsciously setting the stage to do so. He denied it and defended himself for several minutes, as I quietly listened. When he slowed down, I interjected, "I'm sorry, it doesn't wash. You were inflating your big fat alcoholic ego at her expense the entire time." He finally admitted that later in the day he went to a bar and ordered a drink. He had to wait so long to be served that he changed his mind and went to an AA meeting instead.

15. Gets others to play the "blame game"

Having followers is in itself an ego-boosting experience. Inducing disciples to blame other people or classes of persons for their problems is an especially effective way by which to inflate one's ego.

Unfortunately, there is a dearth of credible information

on the drinking and using habits of cult-like leaders. After all, they are among those with the greatest likelihood of suing for libel or slander and whose secrets are most likely to be protected by their enablers. However, there are numerous examples of such leaders in whom alcohol or other drug addiction has proven extremely likely and for whom, therefore, addiction was probably their driving force. Jim Jones, amphetamine and prescription drug addict and likely alcoholic, led 900 men, women and children in Jonestown, Guyana to mass suicide via poisoned Kool-Aid in 1978.[28] Charles E. Dederich convinced a number of AA members to leave and join his cult, known as Synanon. According to its former members, this group engaged in wrongful imprisonment, kidnapping and torture. Dederich had, of course, relapsed long before, even while imposing abstinence on members of this new group.[29] D.C. Stephenson rose to the top of the Ku Klux Klan, creating a political machine that by 1924 controlled Indiana politics. One night he got drunk, raped a woman and was ultimately found responsible for her death.[30] The commission of violence while drinking is a virtual confirmation of alcoholism.

Controlling people to the point at which they commit suicide, torture or simply blame others for the world's (or their ethnicity, social class, gender, etc.) problems is exceptionally ego-inflating. Those in a position to closely observe today's leaders who attempt to account for the problems of a class of people via scapegoats should suspect alcoholism as the motivating force behind the use of such power.

16. Has ever knowingly made a false accusation

As a particularly vile subcategory of lying, falsely

accusing others deserves special attention. In addition, its genesis is borne exclusively in the need to inflate the ego by surreptitious wielding of power over others. Such accusations are made because there is far greater ego-gratification in attacking a person known to be innocent than in assaulting the guilty.[31]

The accusers' heavy alcohol use may have fueled the Salem Witch Trials, as well as similar tragic historic incidents. While conjecture, it fits with the idea that alcoholism causes megalomania and that few non-alcoholics seek to inflate their egos in such deadly ways. Alcoholism could also explain the spate of witch-hunts in the 1980s and early '90s: falsely accusing pre-school teachers of horrifying acts of child abuse.

The McMartin Pre-School case in Manhattan Beach, California is among the most infamous examples. The fact that not one parent had a clue to the abuse the owners, the Buckey family, supposedly committed over a 5-year period should have, by itself, exonerated them. Only a practicing addict could possibly convince others that such activity took place without any solid evidence whatsoever. In fact, 98% of Los Angeles County residents were, at one point during the trial, convinced of the Buckey's guilt, despite the absurdity of the allegations.[32] The original accuser, addict Judy Johnson, committed suicide three years later. By that time, the madness of crowds had taken on a life of its own. However, for a travesty of such magnitude to continue not only beyond an initial allegation, but also for years, alcoholism is extremely likely in one or more of the witnesses for the prosecution and/or prosecutors. Some day, when historians review events with an understanding of addiction, they may find that addicts play an instigating and continuing role in most crowd psychology. (Mobs are ruled by their limbic systems which, aside from being responsible for impulsive behaviors, are also necessary for basic survival. This causes us to follow others when, for example, danger is imminent. It's possible that some alcoholics are so "in touch" with their reptilian brains, they are able to connect with the limbic system in others to a marked degree. This may give them the ability to impel others to engage in behaviors the neo-cortex would normally prevent. When paired with the need to inflate the ego and resulting desire to control others, their power to lead crowds may be unparalleled.) Without understanding addiction and using the scientific method to test hypotheses that alcoholism exists where unsuspected by others, this conclusion may seem absurd. However, comprehending the brain chemistry and consequential ego inflation makes this predictable and, even, logical.

The Buckeys were eventually acquitted. Along the way, a number of prosecutors quit the case because of their belief that the defendants were innocent. A number of people refused to testify for the prosecution.

The addict's environment, circumstances, Temperament and gender influence the kind of attack. Females commit non-violent assaults more frequently due to lack of size and strength. However, given the right situation, such as a political system of capitalism threatened by one of totalitarian socialism, a male may resort to false accusations against any and all political enemies. The alcoholism of Senator Joseph McCarthy, who led the House Un-American Activities Committee in the 1950s in the witch hunt for communists, explains such behavior.

17. Wields power capriciously

W. M. Ireland commented that "Power is nothing if it

be consciously applied. The man who...punishes the guilty, who absolves only the innocent, whose testimony is inexorably true, has no real power at all."[33] There must instead be *abuse* of power.

This can take form in many of the behaviors listed here. The alcoholic may lie to some and not to others, while falsely accusing the innocent. He may charm certain people while intimidating others, for no apparent reason and with no particular pattern. He may incarcerate or kill many top cronies and absolve a few, as Joseph Stalin did. The alcoholic may favor one child over another. In unpredictable fashion, she may alternate abuse with remorse for having mistreated others. The most destructive alcoholics are whimsical in their misuse of power. They engage in many of these behaviors randomly, having no rhyme or reason for their actions. They are erratic and unstable, acting in ways we can't even imagine or fathom. The one prognostication we can make about the practicing addict is that we cannot predict how destructive his behaviors may become, or when.

18. Has ever betrayed another

Active alcoholics excel in vile behaviors. The most loathsome conduct includes false accusations and betrayal.

The various meanings behind the word "betrayal" suggest extraordinary power. These include, "to seduce and fail to marry," a way by which to wield power over the opposite sex. "To mislead, to lead astray," is a form of lying. Consider the power that one may gain over another by disclosing "something intended to be kept secret," or "to break faith with by disclosing a secret," as a friend betraying a confidence. Perhaps the most odious is, "to deliver into the hands of an enemy by treachery or fraud, in violation of trust," as the clearly alcoholic Fernand did to his best friend, Edmond Dantes in the 2001 movie version of the Alexandre Dumas classic, "The Count of Monte Cristo."

To "help the enemy of (one's country, cause, etc.); to be a traitor to," is probably the most far-reaching act of betrayal. In his study of famous alcoholics and their destructive behaviors, James Graham devotes an entire chapter to traitors. Pointing out that everyday treachery among alcoholics is common, it might not be surprising that an "extraordinary number of real traitors...have been alcoholics."[34] He shows that the greatest spy ring in history, four British subjects spying for the KGB during WW-II, consisted of alcoholics. Guy Burgess and Donald Maclean had previously been identified as having alcoholism. Graham painstakingly makes the case that so were Kim Philby and Anthony Blunt. He names several dozen other traitors who had this disease.[35] There is a huge payoff to the alcoholic in terms of being able to inflate the ego when betraying an entire nation-state.

Graham includes in his study of spies Christopher Boyce, whose sordid story was told in the book and movie, "The Falcon and The Snowman." Boyce was known to drink heavily during work hours and was portrayed in the movie as clearly having alcoholism. He masterminded one of the most damaging conspiracies ever perpetrated against the United States, betraying the secrets of a $5 billion defense satellite system in favor of the former Soviet Union.

As is the case for other apprehended criminals, not every traitor is an alcoholic. Former FBI agent Robert Hanssen is probably an exception to the rule.[36] However, since roughly 85% of incarcerated prisoners have this disease, it would be surprising if this were not true for a like percentage of those qualifying for life imprisonment for having violated their country's trust.

19. Has a need to win at any cost

Screen star Bette Davis' adopted daughter, B. D. Hyman, in *My Mother's Keeper*, could only make sense of Davis' behavior by concluding that the one thing tying her conduct together was the need to win, regardless of who she stepped on.[37] However, Hyman didn't understand that this relentless need was rooted, as were her other behaviors, in alcoholism.[38]

Fighting for its own sake and winning is an ego-satiating experience. The subject of the argument is unimportant. It takes different forms in ways determined by the underlying personality of the alcoholic. Some debate ideas and must win such arguments at all costs, ranting and raving until the other party gives up. Others quarrel over property lines and demand that the neighbor should pay the cost of a fence, even though it divides their parcels. Still other alcoholics squabble over an umpire's call at a child's baseball game and fly into a rage over a decision with which he disagrees. Some feud over bloodlines, because that's what their forefathers did. Cooperation or conceding the point is not an option: these do nothing to inflate the ego.

20. Serious problems at home

One of the difficulties in identifying alcoholics is that misbehaviors are often hidden from public view. Sometimes, the alcoholic is destructive only in his closest relationships. Outsiders may be unaware of problems for years, while trouble is brewing.

Many of the behaviors listed, including pontificating, lying, adultery and the need to win at any cost, cause severe troubles at home. Close persons usually experience the brunt of these misbehaviors long before there are serious problems at work. The fact that the alcoholic is often successful in his employment serves only to confuse those closest. It also makes it practically futile to share inside knowledge with others, since they may not believe that there could be personal problems. After all, if he's so good at work, how could he possibly be a troublemaker at home? Few understand that the same inflated ego, in the grand paradox of addiction, causes both sets of behaviors.

21. Intimidates others to get his way

The movie "Scent of a Woman" offers a superb portrayal of alcoholic charm and intimidation. Alternating these techniques, alcoholics such as Lt. Col. Frank Slade can more easily get what they want, when they want it. Since the addict is driven to inflate his ego and may do so through conquest, he will do anything to win. Intimidating others is indicative of the need to win and is, therefore, symptomatic of alcoholism.

22. Engages in "telephonitis"

Graham and Robe each described this behavior as common among alcoholics. The afflicted controls others by attempting to force them to talk during all hours of the day or night, at hours selected by the addict. The recent hue and cry over cell phone users and traffic accidents may be identifying only a symptom. The source of the behavior that compels one to constantly use a cell-phone while driving, especially if engaging in other dangerous behaviors, may well be alcoholism whether or not driving under the influence at the time.

Telephonitis was the most important clue among several suggesting that a person observed one Friday evening might be under the influence. He was talking almost incessantly on his cell phone in the middle of a small-town restaurant, desperately trying to find lodging a hundred miles up the road. He alternated with calls to a business associate back home regarding something about a jewelry purchase. His voice was a bit louder than it should have been and he flirted with the waitresses in-between phone calls. My wife and I left a few minutes after he did, only to see him light a cigar as we walked past his Ford F-150 with the music on full-blast. Since there were a number of clues, however slight, I made a mental note of his license plate.

We left at about the same time. I watched him drive without incident for about 20 miles. When he pulled over in the next town at a bar, even though I had observed no on-road misbehaviors, I decided to report the possibility of a DUI. The next day I heard from the Highway Patrol that, thanks to my report, an officer had trailed him. When the man ran a red light, he was stopped, given a sobriety test and arrested for driving under the influence.

23. Engages in "reverse telephonitis"

The addict controls others by hanging up on them. This is a variation of intimidation, and evokes a high sense of self-importance especially when the addict initiated the phone call.

The first — and only — clue I had to a friend's alcoholism was when he hung up on me several times in succession after calling and screaming profanities. I had never seen him drink. However, figuring the only explanation was alcoholism, I phoned several mutual friends. One finally admitted that his behaviors while drinking had become "a real problem." He went into rehab a few years later.

24. Engages in serial Don Juanism or adultery

Despite Shakespeare's admonition that drinking "provokes the desire, but it takes away the performance,"[39] early stage alcoholics often spend a great deal of time and effort in achieving ego-satiation through serial sexual conquests. Such behavior promotes the ego-inflation needed to fuel alcoholism.

There is no more effective way to wield power over others non-violently than through sexual exploitation. This becomes easier as the physically attractive qualities of the alcoholic increase. Don Juanism, the practice of bedding scores if not hundreds or thousands of partners, is extremely common among those with alcoholism. Unfortunately, beauty after money is the alcoholic's biggest enabler.

Adultery is also common among alcoholics. By no means are all adulterers addicts, any more than are all smokers. On the other hand, if a person commits adultery or other violations of contract or trust, the likelihood of uncovering active alcoholism increases by probably a similar factor as when there is smoking, if not a bit more. However, finding, say, a 50% probability of alcoholism when a trust is violated does not mean that five out of ten people who act in this way will prove to have alcoholism. It means instead that we may find alcoholism in 50% of incidents in which a trust is violated. This is very different and takes into account the fact that the alcoholic engages in such behavior far more often than does the non-alcoholic. Therefore, out of 100 acts of adultery, scores of individuals probably acted improperly once, maybe twice. A few may have done so a dozen times or more. The latter are very likely alcoholics. If any of them are not afflicted with alcoholism, they may have been deeply affected by it. I have observed that children of alcoholics often engage in inappropriate conduct, including both Don Juanism and serial adultery, in an effort to compensate for psychological abandonment by a parent.

A very few commit rape. Since, as we will find, most incarcerated criminals are addicts, the vast majority of those committing the atrocity of rape have alcoholism. Rape is a crime not of sex, but of control. Most, thankfully, prefer to control via non-violent means, but this does not lessen the long-term psychological damage experienced by the victim.

25. Hates others

The fact that the addict can do or say nothing wrong suggests that he is blameless for anything that may go wrong in his life or in the lives of those around him. If he is not to blame, who is? Others are, of course. This can lead to resenting and, even, hating them.

Due to euphoric recall and the self-favoring light in which the addict views himself, alcoholism sometimes results in extreme hatred. The most repulsive form of such hatred may be racism. Therefore, it's possible that much racism is rooted in alcoholism. A sober and recalcitrant former Black Panther, Eldridge Cleaver, realized, "If people had listened to Huey Newton and me in the 1960s, there would have been a holocaust in this country."[40] A friend of Governor and sometimes-racist George Wallace reported that "'One drink would set him off on a drunk...(and he) wasn't a very pleasant drunk, either...He became belligerent, wanting to fight anything that moved.'"[41] Although he drank on few occasions, apparently when he did, he lost control over his behaviors. He stopped completely when he realized, "It will cause him to lose control of himself...and something bad will happen."[42] He died "not drinking," with huge support among Blacks. In a variation of hatred, alcoholic-actress Bette Davis despised men, calling them utterly useless, "the shits," and other foul language. While a few cites do not prove the case, one is hard-pressed to find an example of a person filled with such feelings in whom we do not find numerous other signs of alcoholism.

26. Verbally abuses others

Most alcoholics avoid incarceration for criminal acts because they do not commit physical violence against others. Instead, they perpetrate psychological violence through verbal abuse.

Almost every story of an alcoholic involves such attacks, since they are relatively "safe" ways to inflate the ego at the expense of others. By engaging in such mistreatment, the addict is suggesting, "I'm more important and better than you." Hearing someone make belittling and disparaging remarks of another is often a first clue to alcoholism.

27. Physically abuses others

Maria Roy, founder and executive director of Abused Women's Aid in Crisis, Inc., found that 85% of violent husbands had an alcohol or other drug problem.[43] These men did not have to be under the influence when committing a violent act; "very often, the assaults came during sobriety or when the effects of hard drugs had worn off."[44] She also noted that the most common drug used was alcohol.

Men who have been apprehended for domestic violence are often sent to "anger management" classes, where they are taught how to control their temper. The trouble is, many men who are accused of committing such abuse are victims of false accusations and may have themselves suffered assaults by the accusers. The rest likely need treatment for alcoholism, before which the behaviors cannot improve. Evidence for this can be found in several studies showing zero difference in the treatment of women by men between those who had completed domestic violence counseling programs and others, attending no course.[45] One counseling center reported that although it had counseled physical abusers for several years, they had seen only one recovery. These observations suggest that such programs treat symptoms and not their underlying cause.

28. Commits heinous crimes

While most alcoholics never commit a serious crime, there are relatively few non-alcoholics who engage in such acts. Persons evincing numerous behavioral indications of alcoholism have perpetrated most infamous random acts of senseless violence. These include Sam Sheppard, O.J. Simpson, Jeremy Strohmeyer and Abraham Lincoln's killer, John Wilkes Booth. Practically all serial- and mass-murderers, including Richard Speck, Ted Bundy, John Wayne Gacy and Jeffrey L. Dahmer, have been alcoholics. The most tyrannical dictators in world history have also mostly been alcohol or other drug addicts. Joseph Stalin, responsible for the deaths of 30-50 million of his fellow Soviets, was an alcoholic. Adolf Hitler was an amphetamine and barbiturate addict. Chairman Mao Zedong of China, indirectly responsible for the starvation of an estimated 30 million Chinese peasants, was addicted to barbiturates. Hitler's chief henchman, Adolf Eichmann had alcoholism, as did Benito Mussolini.[46] Evidence that Saddam Hussein may be an alcoholic can be found in Con Coughlin's 2002 biography, *Saddam: King of Terror*. It's unlikely that Coughlin would have described this ruthless dictator as "The whiskey-drinking Saddam" in the prologue, unless whiskey is an important part of his life.[47] Biographers just don't usually refer in this way to a subject who only nurses the occasional after-dinner drink.

The megalomaniac alcoholic may commit particularly heinous crimes. Such behaviors contribute to the ego-inflation needed to fuel addiction. Therefore, any act that furthers and maintains power over others, especially if repeated, is an excellent clue to alcoholism. The confusing aspect is that not only do such behaviors vary greatly but, also, the perpetrator may not be under the influence at the time of the crime. Since there is so much in this field about which we cannot obtain direct statistics, we need to extrapolate from what we can. Alcoholics commit about 85% of all felonies. Many have no drugs in their system when the crime is committed. Considering how high-functioning those with early-stage alcoholism can be, there is no reason to exclude from our radar those who engage in well-planned, well orchestrated or particularly monstrous criminal acts.

Support for this hypothesis can be found in Graham's idea that egomania borne of alcoholism does not disappear when the drinking stops. The bloated ego must also be simultaneously deflated. This is consistent with the fact that the 12-Step program is designed to deflate the ego. Graham suggests that these "power symptoms" disappear "*only* if the drinking stops and the bloated ego is deflated."[48] Evidence for the idea that the process usually begins almost immediately in a program of sobriety is found in a study reporting the percentage of early-recovery alcoholics scoring sociopathic on the psychopathological indicator, the MMPI (Minnesota Multiphasic Personality Inventory.) The portion plummeted from over 90% to less than 10% in just 25 days.[49] On the other hand, many alcoholics become abstinent for long periods without undergoing ego-deflation (usually via Alcoholics Anonymous or some similar program, which are designed to deflate that ego). This could account for the rare instance of sociopathic behavior committed by alcoholics who may not have been drinking for months or even years.

While alcoholics may commit unspeakable acts when under the influence, those in the middle-to-latter stages may be most visibly sick in-between uses. Milam and Ketcham point out, "When the alcoholic stops drinking, all hell breaks loose. Blood vessels constrict, cutting down on the flow of blood and oxygen to the cells. The blood glucose level drops sharply and remains unstable. The [levels of] brain amines, serotonin and norepinephrine, decrease dramatically. Hormones, enzymes, and body fluid levels fluctuate erratically....The resulting pandemonium creates numerous psychological and physiological problems for the alcoholic, including profound mental confusion, memory defects...paranoia, violent or fearful behavior...."[50] No wonder we are unable to link addiction to criminal activity. Often, the crime occurs while the addict is not under the influence, when suffering is at its worst.

5

A Sense of Invincibility

1. Engages in unnecessarily reckless behaviors

The assumption of extraordinary risks allows ego inflation to occur in front of often-supportive family, friends and fans. Recovering alcoholics inform us that their emotional growth stopped the day they triggered alcoholism. Since the average age at which this occurs is 13, the grown-up alcoholic is, emotionally, an adolescent. He has a child's sense of invincibility and wants to show others, "look at what I can do," or even, "look at what I can get away with." Successfully engaging in such acts further fuels that ego, reinforcing the sense of invincibility. In the case of addicts, this can result in increasingly reckless behavior.

The Supreme Being complex is probably behind extraordinarily risky behaviors that serve a useful purpose. A sense of invincibility likely explains most such conduct that is unnecessary, such as driving on a windy, mountain road without a seat restraint, or doing 90 mph in a 30-mph zone.

Non-addicts may subject themselves to the consequences of reckless behaviors they would never impose on others. Addicts often won't hesitate to act recklessly at the expense of strangers. They'll even risk sacrificing family and friends. Financial or sexual escapades that subject close persons to excessive monetary gambles or health hazards are commonplace in the progression of alcoholism. Failing to strap an infant or small child in a vehicle exemplifies the taking of risks with the lives of others, but also may be a sign of the impaired judgment that indicates latter-stage alcoholism or polydrug addiction. Two-thirds of alcohol-related vehicular fatalities among child passengers are the result of DUI by the child's driver, often a parent.[51] If other drivers were to observe unbelted child passengers and take appropriate action with follow-through by authorities, many of these tragedies might be averted.

2. Involved in an accident, especially multiple mishaps

Poor judgment takes its toll in middle to latter stage addiction, but the feeling that they can do anything inevitably leads to a higher rate of accidents among early-stage alcoholics than for others. A National Highway Traffic Safety Administration (NHTSA) study reported specific on-road behaviors and probabilities of driving under the influence (DUI).[52] Many of the misbehaviors the study found as indicative of DUI are signs of impaired judgment and apparent mental confusion, which represent the more obvious drunks. For now, we are primarily concerned with the early-stage alcoholic who would have been able to avoid the impending accident were it not for the fact that he thinks he's invincible.

Symptoms denoting a sense of invincibility include tailgating, which was found to be associated with DUIs in 50% of all cases, and turning with excessive speed, which was effected by a driver under the influence about 35% of the time. Other signs include such maneuvers as passing on a two-lane highway over a solid yellow line, failing to buckle up and speeding recklessly through traffic, as well as excessive speed in inclement weather, including fog, snow and cloudbursts.

Accidents may also be a result of acting out on the supreme-being complex. The NHTSA study found that making obscene gestures while driving was linked to DUI in 60% of such cases. When we think someone is just having a "bad day," we might want to think again. Those not yielding the right of way, such as cutting in line, were DUI 45% of the time. While littering, driving alone in a carpool lane, parking in a handicapped space without a disability or unnecessarily taking up two parking spaces may be considered indications of someone who believes he is the Supreme Being, these either failed to indicate at least a 30% probability of DUI, or were not measured in the study. However, we would note that even a 20% likelihood of DUI is several times the average in the driving population at the time of day during which the study was conducted (nighttime, when an average of 5% of drivers are DUI). And, these other bouts of poor conduct might be found in the alcoholic in-between drinking episodes, ego intact.

Poor judgment accounts for a number of accidents, since the following behaviors indicated a probability of DUI of at least 45%: one set of tires on a line, straddling the line, driving on the shoulder, abruptly swerving, drifting, unnecessary braking and backing into traffic. Apparent mental confusion is also the proximate cause of many incidents. Behaviors indicating such confusion, coinciding with DUI at least 45% of the time, included: driving straight in the turn-only lane without turning, moving slower than 10 mph below the speed limit, erratic braking, and driving the wrong way down a one-way street. DUIs were found in at least 30% of the following behaviors: stopping inappropriately, making an illegal or abrupt turn, turning from outside a designated turn lane, and headlights not on when required. Note that a number of the driving behaviors listed could be accounted for by a sense of invincibility or Supreme Being complex, including backing into traffic and driving straight in the turn-only lane.

"Almost striking an object or vehicle" at night, which is probably best linked to poor judgment, indicated a 60% probability of DUI. Considering the fact that the percent of fatalities that can be connected to DUIs are about 40%, why would "actually" striking an object or vehicle be far from 40-60%? A number of Drug Recognition Experts interviewed suggest that published statistics on non-fatal accidents (which, amazingly, report that as few as 7% of such incidents are related to DUI) probably seriously understate the problem. They believe that the odds of DUI in such cases are probably 40-50%. (These DREs also feel that both parties involved in accidents are frequently DUI because sober drivers are often able to avoid such incidents.)

The well-known on-road alcohol-related fatality figure of 40% (about 16,000 out of 40,000 deaths per year) could be low. In fatal accidents, only 75% of drivers are tested for alcohol and none for other drugs. Yet, the NHTSA's Field Validation Study of the Drug Recognition Expert program found that less than 4% of the suspects who had used other psychoactive drugs had a BAL of .10 per cent or greater.[53] In other words, among suspects using drugs other than alcohol, over 96% were found not legally drunk. Some DREs believe that for every three or four DUIs under the influence of alcohol, at least one more is under the influence of other drugs with little or no alcohol in his system.

Considering the fact that drugs "potentiate" each other, resulting in a far more powerful punch than any one drug provides (i.e., relatively little of each drug, when combined, does the trick), the fatalities resulting from DUI may be substantially higher than suspected. It would not be surprising if they are closer to the 60% of drivers that the NHTSA study found under the influence when objects or other vehicles were "almost struck."

We find similar numbers in non-road incidents. The percent of drowning deaths attributable to alcohol is estimated at 70%, while 90% of fatalities from fire involve alcohol.[54] Various workplace studies have shown 50-90% of on-the-job accidents are related to alcohol. Such events declined by 82% after treating employees identified as having alcoholism at the Lansing, Michigan, Oldsmobile plant.[55] Similarly, a study of snowmobile accidents in Wisconsin reported that as many as 70% were related to the equivalent of DUIs among snowmobile drivers. Other studies have found that addicts are five times more likely than non-addicts to file worker's compensation claims.[56] Addicts were also found to be 3.6 times more likely to injure themselves or another person in the workplace and also deemed responsible for about 40% of all industrial fatalities (a statistic remarkably similar to driving casualties).[57] As Father Martin and other great alcoholism experts have pointed out, if alcohol causes problems then the problem is alcohol.[58]

That a person drives or swims while under the influence suggests a sense of invincibility, or he wouldn't engage in such a potentially dangerous activity while in that condition. The fact that he works while stoned indicates that he doesn't believe he is more likely to err or get caught. This accounts for the inclusion of accidents in the category suggesting a mindset that one is invincible, even though the proximate cause of many accidents may very often be poor judgment or mental confusion. However, the root of the distorted perceptions is the same: alcohol or other drug addiction.

3. Drives while under the influence

Countless recovering alcoholics tell us they would drink beyond the legal limit, drive, have a scare and vow "never again." Yet, almost all of them repeatedly broke that vow before entering recovery.

Even though he may have the best of intentions when he begins drinking, as the blood alcohol level rises, the person with alcoholism begins to experience the distortion of euphoric recall, which serves as internal feedback that he can do no wrong. If so, surely he can drive. And, according to recovering addicts, he does so an average of 80 times per year in a condition in which he should not.

At best, the person committing this offense is apprehended only once in every 500 incidents and at worst, one in every 2,000. He is caught, then, just once in every six to 24 years.

In contrast to the person with alcoholism, the non-alcoholic does not think that he is invincible. Because he knows he is human, he rarely, if ever, drinks beyond the legal limit and gets behind the wheel of a car. On the other hand, he will more readily show the classic signs of inebriation. While walking, this may be a staggered gait. When driving, this translates to weaving and similar driver errors.

The highly tolerant early-stage alcoholic can reach a BAL as high as .24 per cent before he staggers and, therefore, weaves. Yet often, he drives when his BAL is between .10 and .20 per cent. He is not only rarely stopped, but even when he is, traffic officers fail to arrest him for DUI most of the time.

This was proven in a Fort Lauderdale, Florida, study in which traffic violators, apprehended by police but not suspected of DUI, were ready to get back on the road. Researchers then administered breath tests to these drivers. We would think that the researchers might find two or three DUIs for every ten the officers arrested. After all, the officers were up close and personal, able to smell the breath of the offender and look at his eyes at close range. The questions officers traditionally ask are designed to confuse. "May I see your drivers' license, along with proof of insurance and registration," is quickly followed by queries such as, "Sir, where are you headed to tonight?" It is thought that a DUI will lose track and be unable to follow such multi-tasking directions.

Unfortunately, this is not the case for the early-stage highly tolerant person with alcoholism. If it were, the researchers would have found just two or three more DUIs for every ten the officers found. They didn't stop at five or ten, or twenty or thirty. They found thirty-seven DUIs for every ten the officers arrested. In other words, highly trained police officers identified only 21% of those later proven to be DUI at a time when the legal limit for BAL was .10 per cent, even after close personal contact.

If highly trained police officers are unable to detect alcohol on the breath, see it in the eyes or recognize it in the behavior, what are the odds the close person will find it? This is a terrific study to keep in mind when friends tell others who have been victimized by addicts, "you should have been able to see the drug use." How could they, when the vast majority of police officers fail to detect it? Also consider this when attempting to have someone pulled over for on-road misbehaviors. The public might consider demanding that every traffic violator be tested for blood alcohol level using a simple non-intrusive eye test that takes any trained officer less than a minute to administer. This test, called Horizontal Gaze Nystagmus, or HGN, requires holding the head straight while tracking a finger from side to side. The angle of deviation from straight ahead at which point an involuntary shaking of the eyeballs begins to occur determines the BAL. Any trained police officer can determine this within .02 per cent in a timeframe of about 30 seconds. This could help solve the DUI problem. It also may be the single most effective way to coerce abstinence and force many alcoholics into a program of sobriety.

In the days of MADD, the odds of alcoholism in a person convicted once of DUI are extremely high. If a non-alcoholic is convicted (or even accused), he will vow to never again repeat this behavior, and keep the promise. Only a person having a sense of invincibility rooted in alcoholism is likely to perpetrate this crime again.

4. Has committed a felony

A sense of invincibility rooted in alcoholism, often combined with a "supreme being" complex, may result in most felonious behavior. (Or it would, if addicts didn't have to steal in order to be able to afford illegal drugs. Such behavior is commonplace only because of legal proscriptions, just as it was during Prohibition. The commission of felonies is therefore far more common among latter-stage or polydrug addicts than would be the case if such drugs were decriminalized.) The kind of violations differ depending upon underlying personality type, virulence of the disease, the degree of buildup of acetaldehyde on the brain, and circumstances/environment. Alcoholics attending Beverly Hills High probably commit different kinds of violations than do those growing up in a ghetto.

Journalists reporting on criminal behavior rarely comment on alcohol or other drug "problems" in alleged or convicted felons. If they note anything, it's usually in the 28th paragraph of a story. Since few are aware of the role that alcohol plays in the behavior, they generally don't look for it and, therefore, have nothing to report. If they mention it at all, the placement in the story is suggestive of the idea that the suspect is innately bad. Bad people, of course, use drugs.

Reports of possible alcohol or other drug use, not to mention addiction, is even more infrequent in stories of upper-class criminals. Barry Minkow's use probably would likely have been ignored were it not for his notoriety. Minkow, an over-achiever showing behavioral signs of addiction (megalomania) defrauded those who invested in his carpet cleaning company, ZZZZ Best, out of a hundred million dollars. According to reports, he sold cocaine to continue funding what was essentially a Ponzi scheme.[59] At barely 20 years of age, he exhibited none of the commonly recognized signs of alcoholism, although several of his associates appear to have been well beyond the early-stage. However, Minkow did use illegal drugs other than marijuana, which is strongly suggestive of addiction. Non-addicts, once out of school (where drug use is so rampant that we cannot distinguish between addict and non-addict), rarely use such drugs. Those not having alcoholism usually lack the sense of invincibility required to take such risks with the law.

The white-collar alcoholic is also better protected. Recall that the higher the person's social, business, professional or political status, the greater the enabling (protection from consequences) on the part of close persons, because the enablers have so much to lose. While enablers make an unequivocal diagnosis of addiction difficult, the commission of a felony in itself greatly increases the odds of alcoholism.

Every recovering addict ex-con interviewed for this and prior books has felt that 90% or more of their fellow prisoners were alcoholics. Another wrote, in the "Big Book" of Alcoholics Anonymous, "If everyone [could be in AA], there would be no need for jails."[60] Where we dig deep enough, we find signs of alcohol or other drug addiction in practically every burglary, theft, homicide and even white-collar crime such as embezzlement, or accounting and securities fraud.

We have been taught to look for symptoms of latter-stage alcoholism, when the afflicted is less competent at most endeavors, including criminal behaviors. The early-stage alcoholic is least suspected, more competent and, therefore, potentially far more dangerous. Combining the need to over-achieve with an ability to tell lies that even juries may believe, they are amazingly capable of convincing others, especially the more gullible among us, into committing their deeds. Though probably not early-stage alcoholics, the antagonists in the book and movie, "A Simple Plan," suggested the commission of murders into which a non-addict allowed himself to be drawn. This illustrates the extraordinary psychological power the addict often wields over others, as well as the risks in failing to understand, identify and treat alcoholism at the earliest possible stage.

Hundreds of thousands of prisoners are undiagnosed and untreated alcoholics. We might reflect on the likelihood that while monstrous behaviors led to their incarceration, these convicts could be fundamentally good people. We can greatly reduce the risks of subsequent criminal behavior by identifying and intervening near the outset in the development of alcoholism. We might also consider the possibility that it's never too late for redemption and doing more to coerce abstinence in all inmates.

6

Physical Signs of Early-Stage Alcoholism

1. Has an ethnic background with a higher risk of alcoholism

As politically incorrect as this may seem, if we want to help people, we need to stop ignoring the differences in the rate of alcoholism between those of varied ethnic backgrounds and instead, *explain* the disparity.

African-Americans, totaling only 12% of the American population, comprise 40% of prison inmates. Rather than suggesting that this racial group consists of more "bad" people than do those of other ancestries, or that white cops are more likely to arrest non-whites, we might consider the possibility that people of certain ancestries have a greater genetic predisposition to alcoholism than do others.

James R. Milam may have been among the first to suggest a role of ancestry in determining the biological likelihood of alcoholism.[61] He noted that there is an amazing correlation between the level of alcoholism and period of time during which peoples have had access to large quantities of alcohol. He hypothesized that a high rate of alcoholism results in a resistance to it, perhaps a result of early demise among those with alcoholic genes. Southern Europeans, including the Greeks, Jews and Southern Italians, who have had such availability for 10,000 to 15,000 years, experience the lowest rates of alcoholism, estimated at 5%. Northern Europeans by contrast, including Russians, Scandinavians and the Irish, have had access for only 1,200-1,500 years. The rate of alcoholism in these population groups is far greater, believed to be 20% to 30%. Native Americans have had this access for only 100-400 years, zero time on a micro-evolutionary scale to result in a resistance to this disease. Regardless of the climate in which they live, such Americans experience epidemic rates, reportedly as high as 75% on some reservations. Similarly, it is not likely that those in Black Africa had access to alcohol in sufficient quantities and for a long enough period of time to build immunity to alcoholism.

To suggest that alcoholism is a behavioral disorder is to disparage entire classes of people, including Native Americans, Irish, Russians and African Americans. Alcoholism is not caused by bad conduct. Alcoholism causes poor behaviors, including criminal actions. It's time to treat prisoners of all races for alcoholism so that after the consequences for their misbehaviors are meted out, they can leave prison and lead productive and worthwhile lives, instead of being predestined to repeat the behaviors that resulted in their incarceration.

2. Has a parent or child with alcoholism

In a pivotal study,[62] Dr. Donald Goodwin demolished the idea that alcoholism is learned behavior or that its inception has anything to do with environmental influences (other than availability). He found that adopted out children of alcoholics experienced a rate of alcoholism almost four times that of a control group of adopted children whose biological parents were not alcoholics. The children of alcoholics had no exposure to their alcoholic parent after the first few weeks of life, thereby removing environmental influences. This occurred despite the fact that the adoptive parents in the control group had almost twice the rate of alcoholism as the adoptive parents of the biological children of alcoholics group.

In another part of the study, Goodwin compared sons of alcoholics adopted out with brothers raised by their alcoholic families. There was no difference in the incidence of alcoholism between the two groups of brothers. The rate of alcoholism was, again, almost four times that of a control group. This is consistent with the idea of genetic susceptibility observable in different ancestries, and accounts for the observation that alcoholism is far more common in some families than in others.

The fact that there is less than a 100% rate of alcoholism does not mean the disease is not passed through in the genes. Children of diabetics are far more likely to develop diabetes than others, but not all do so. This is also true for a number of other diseases, including sickle-cell anemia.

These findings also suggest the reverse: a child who is an alcoholic is more likely to have an alcoholic parent. Two studies of women alcoholics, in which 41% and 49% had at least one alcoholic parent, support this idea.[63] Usually we find alcoholism in the parent long before we see it in a child, but occasionally the opposite is true, especially in the case of polydrug use by the child and only alcohol use in the parent.

Although no studies could be found, anecdotal support is strong that alcoholism runs in the extended family.

Alcoholism in a grandparent or in aunts and uncles may substantially increase the odds that a child of non-alcoholic parents will inherit this disease.

3. Drinks champagne and certain other drinks

Addicts excel at finding ways of accelerating the release of drugs into the system. The carbonation in champagne or soda water results in a quicker increase in blood alcohol level by more quickly opening the pyloric valve into the small intestine, making the absorption more rapid, than it would otherwise be. Mixed drinks may arouse some additional suspicion as well, since alcoholics can more easily hide the amount of alcohol in such drinks, often making them far stronger than a single shot.

4. Drinks heavily on empty stomach

Persons with alcoholism drink to get drunk, even if they happen to like the taste. Food in the stomach delays the absorption of alcohol, while drinking on an empty stomach helps to quicken the assimilation into the blood stream. Many recovering alcoholics inform us that they drank before eating near the start of their drinking career. As the alcoholism progresses, some report getting most of their calories from alcohol by eating less or hardly at all.

5. Seems to always be having "a party" or going to one

Alcoholics want their drug readily available without too many questions. "Party boys" and "party girls" are often early-stage alcohol and other drug addicts. Everyone else is using, making it easy to identify acquaintances as alcoholics, thereby shifting the focus. Besides, parties are great places to inflate the ego through Don Juanism.

A lighter-weight version of this may be inventing social occasions for drinking, such as inviting friends for lunch, cocktails or dinner. The alcoholic will never admit to using these as alibis for drinking. Even an objective, aware observer may see many such occasions and think nothing of it. He should think again.

6. Gulps his or her liquor

If a person wants to get drunk, there's no more efficient way than to gulp a few shots of hard liquor. Even recovering alcoholics who drank only wine admit that the first few glasses often "just disappeared."

On the other hand, we may never see gulping. If he "pre-drank," which is defined as drinking in private, usually alone before a social or business event, we won't have a clue to alcoholism by watching him drink. We are likely to observe a person under scrutiny sip, which serves only to confuse. Yet the arithmetic of "maintenance drinking," maintaining a given blood alcohol level, is not only illuminating but also amazing.

Once a person reaches a desired blood alcohol level (BAL), very little additional alcohol is necessary to stay at this level. While weight and other factors play a role in the rate of increase of BAL, the body assimilates the drug at about .015 per cent per hour, regardless of such factors. Since a 120-pound person increases her BAL by .03 per cent per drink (as defined), she requires only half a drink per hour to offset her body's assimilation. She needs, then, only three-quarters of an ounce of 80-proof liquor, 2.5 ounces of wine or 6 ounces of beer per hour to remain at a given BAL. Few food and drink servers or even bartenders come close to guessing that such a miniscule amount of alcohol is required for maintenance drinking.

Figure 1
Blood Alcohol Level/Weight Chart[64]

*No of Drinks	Body Weight in Pounds								
	100	120	140	160	180	200	220	240	
1	0.04	0.03	0.03	0.02	0.02	0.02	0.02	0.02	Not Legally Under
2	0.08	0.06	0.05	0.05	0.04	0.04	0.03	0.03	the Influence
3	0.11	0.09	0.08	0.07	0.06	0.06	0.05	0.05	Driving Ability
4	0.15	0.12	0.11	0.09	0.08	0.08	0.07	0.06	Impaired
5	0.19	0.16	0.13	0.12	0.11	0.09	0.09	0.08	and
6	0.23	0.19	0.16	0.14	0.13	0.11	0.1	0.09	Dangerous
7	0.26	0.22	0.19	0.16	0.15	0.13	0.12	0.11	Definitely Under
8	0.3	0.25	0.21	0.19	0.17	0.17	0.14	0.13	the Influence
9	0.34	0.28	0.24	0.21	0.19	0.19	0.15	0.14	and
10	0.38	0.31	0.27	0.23	0.21	0.19	0.17	0.16	Deadly

HOW TO USE THE CHART

1. Determine your weight category (use the lower weight if you fall between two categories.)
2. Determine the number of drinks you will have, or have, consumed.
3. Subract .015 per cent BAL per hour of drinking

Example: A person weighing 160 lbs. drinking six beers in three hours would have a BAL level of approximately .09%. This amount is significant and will cause judgment errors. Considered "legally" intoxicated in many states.

One "drink" is a 12-ounce bottle of beer, a 5-ounce glass of wine, or 1.5 ounces of 80 proof liquor.

A 200-pound person increases his BAL by .02 per cent per drink. He requires just three-fourths of a drink per hour, or barely over an ounce of liquor, 3.75 ounces of wine or 9 ounces of beer to stay at the same BAL. This isn't nearly enough to cause anyone to inquire about possible alcoholism. Not only do plenty of non-alcoholics drink at a rate greater than this, but also these are quantities at which a teetotaler who starts with nothing in his system can drink and maintain a BAL of near zero.

Nor are we likely to easily diagnose those who combine alcohol with other drugs. An addict can, as previously noted, combine small amounts of different drugs and achieve a far greater effect than merely one drug at twice the level. On the other hand, gulping without follow-through (continuing to drink excessively) may be a clue to other drugs on board.

7. Has high tolerance

The non-alcoholic has never been taught or trained to count the drinks. In fact, Al-Anon (the counterpart to Alcoholics Anonymous, intended for spouses and other close persons of alcoholics) may be construed to teach that those who count have a problem with controlling others. Instead, it might help its members to understand that they need to not only keep track and calculate the BAL, but also when alcoholism is confirmed offer a choice of sobriety or a restraining order to the person under scrutiny.

Elizabeth Taylor provides a terrific example of an extraordinary achiever with alcoholic tolerance. The fact of several marriages before entering the Betty Ford Clinic in 1983 for pill dependency would alert us budding Alcohol and other Drug Addiction Recognition Experts to probable alcoholism. In fact, she realized that she was "also" an alcoholic two weeks into her stay at the Clinic. She could, by her own testimony, "drink anybody under the table and never get drunk." The term "get drunk" when used in this context clearly means "exhibit the normal signs of inebriation," i.e., slurred speech, staggered gait, etc. Richard Burton, also an alcoholic, "almost drank himself into oblivion, in a futile attempt to keep up with Elizabeth."[65]

Early-stage alcoholics don't develop high tolerance. Because of the slow conversion of acetaldehyde to acetate, they are born with it. While the typical teetotaler may show classic signs of inebriation at a blood alcohol level as low as .05 per cent, those with early-stage alcoholism may not appear "drunk" until their BAL is as high as .24 per cent. This, unfortunately, was true for Princess Diana's driver, Henri Paul.

The hotel video prior to the tragedy in which both were killed showed an apparently sober Paul. No one who saw him in the video could have guessed that not only had he been drinking, but also that his BAL was .178 per cent. A 200-pound person requires the equivalent of two bottles of wine over four hours to reach this level. That would knock out most non-alcoholics.

Yet, no one seemed to know his secret. This is the reason the rest of us need to share information about those who may have alcoholism. The difficulty in confirming a diagnosis with only our own observations may be best understood by analogy: alcoholics are like icebergs, with 90% of what's really going on lying beneath the surface, behind closed doors. We each see the visible 10% from our own vantagepoint and observe a different piece of the puzzle. Some of us may see mostly charmers and achievers, with little of the negative side of alcoholism. To get an idea of the destructive potential, we need to cooperate with one another. The alcoholic will likely call it "conspiracy." In reality, it may be the only way to prevent tragedy.

PART III

Middle-Stage or Polydrug Clues

Although displaying multiple symptoms of early-stage alcoholism, most alcoholics are not identified as such until well into the progression of their disease. Father Joseph Martin suggests that it can take about nine years on average for a spouse to begin tentatively diagnosing alcoholism in the other spouse. It probably takes another ten or twenty years for the average non-alcoholic spouse to share suspicions with outsiders. No one is served by keeping the family secrets, yet the stigma of alcoholism precludes discussion, without which a confirmed diagnosis may be impossible.

While few are identified with certainty as having alcoholism up to this point, it is hoped that middle-stage clues — if it's gotten this far — will resolve any doubts.

7

Poor Judgment

1. Under-achiever

The opposite of over-achievement may be a great clue to latter-stage alcoholism or, especially, polydrug addiction. It has not gone unnoticed that a common sign of marijuana addiction is underachievement, although this seems to occur less at the expense of others than of the addict himself.

As the brain's ability to produce its own neurotransmitters is declining, the addict becomes more obsessed with obtaining his drug. Other interests and activities gradually go by the wayside. Under-achievement, except where required to maintain access to the drug, is the inevitable result. Many of the following symptoms are indicative of or contribute to such failure, both at work and at home.

2. Plays the "blame game"

The alcoholic experience of euphoric recall, compelling him to remember everything in a self-favoring light, leads to abrogation of responsibility. If he does or says nothing bad or wrong, how can he be to blame for anything? He cannot.

The immature non-addict will sometimes fall into this trap, delaying self-improvement. If not a disciple of one who convinces others to play the game, this habit is usually broken. Repeated instances, however, should arouse suspicions of likely alcohol or other drug addiction.

Players of this game are incapable of being criticized without shifting blame, or making a mistake without blaming someone else. Not everyone who sues a fast-food restaurant for dropping hot coffee in her lap has addiction, but those who sue bicycle manufacturers for being injured while riding at night without lights may well be afflicted with this disease. The same is likely true for someone slapping an employer with a wrongful termination suit, even though they were excessively absent or late. In other words, plaintiffs who we might think would know better than to engage in a particular conduct, or who blame others despite repeated instances of poor behaviors, are far more likely to have addiction than are those who accept responsibility.

Plaintiffs may blame others and sue in an effort to wield power (too often successfully, by winning their cases). Some of these, especially those who win and, therefore, successfully inflate their egos, may be in early-stage alcoholism. On the other hand, it usually takes an error in judgment to have gone to court as a plaintiff in the sort of case to which we are referring.

According to those social workers who have some degree of knowledge about alcoholism, 80-90% of all welfare recipients are also substance addicts. The rest, are likely their victims. We might observe that just as an enabler robs the addict of the wherewithal to rebuild his self-esteem by repeatedly rescuing him, society robs the wel-

fare recipient of this ability through institutionalized res-
cues, euphemistically referred to as "putting a floor" under
him. Since the welfare recipient has only limited opportunities to inflate his ego, even if young he is probably in the
middle-to-latter stages of his disease.

3. Has unreasonable resentments

This is among the few specifically named character
defects mentioned at AA meetings that those in recovery
admit to while practicing alcoholics. Since blaming others
for one's problems can lead to resentments this clue is, like
so many, rooted in euphoric recall.

The poor, especially, often resent the rich, as if another
person's riches caused them to be poor. But no matter, the
wealthy are terrific scapegoats. This clue is so common that
it ceases to be a good one in many cases of mob uprisings.
However, those who lead the mob and blame others for
their plight, fueling unreasonable resentments, may have
early-stage alcoholism. The followers are, often, either
middle- to latter-stage alcoholics or codependent children
of addicts who have not yet grown up. Responsibility is
not something that practicing alcoholics and sometimes,
even their progeny, easily accept.

4. Makes repeated promises to never do "it" again, whatever "it" may be.

"It" refers to any negative behavior including drinking
and abusing others. The promises are repeated because the
subject does it again and again. For example, he repeatedly promises to stop drinking and driving, or never again to
physically abuse his family. Such promises are, of course,
hollow, when addiction continues unimpeded.

5. Has a poor reputation (personally or professionally)

"Is drinking affecting your reputation?" is one of AA's twenty questions[66] to assist the alcoholic in self-diagnosis. Unfortunately, as pointed out elsewhere,[67] these questions are useful only when the alcoholic has hit bottom, which is a rare event in the life of the practicing addict. The questions allow for rationalizations, such as, "My reputation has nothing to do with my drinking. I was set up for failure by my friend/employer/spouse/employee."

Generally of course, a reputation is going downhill among peers at school ("she's easy") or at work ("he makes too many mistakes") because of poly-drug or middle-to-latter stage addiction. Successful ego-inflation requires minimizing the sort of errors that allow a bad reputation to develop. As a result, we rarely see this in early-stage alcoholism.

6. Has very loose sexual morals

This is serial Don Juanism run amuck. Many, if not most, prostitutes are addicts, as is probably the case for triple-x rated adult film stars. (Many of those who are not addicts may be children of alcoholics, attempting to compensate for psychological abandonment by the alcoholic parent.) The further along the addiction or the greater the extent of polydrug use, the lower the companions on the socioeconomic scale and the more X-rated the behavior likely becomes. However, the fact that the addict becomes increasingly less attractive as addiction progresses may eventually result in a decrease in the level of promiscuity.

7. Has been married/divorced several times

One alcoholism authority estimates that 50 to 70% of all

divorces involve alcoholism.[68] Although this may be a high estimate, consider the fact that many alcoholics are married a number of times. It's similar in principle to the National Highway Traffic Safety Administration finding that 35% of illegal turns involve a DUI. Many of us occasionally commit such misdemeanors, but alcoholics do so far more frequently than do others. Lucy Barry Robe found that 86% of famous women in a sample group of addict women had been divorced at least once (the average percentage of marriages *ending* in divorce in the U.S. population hovers somewhere near 50%) and 45% were married at least three times, which applies to only 16% of all women in the U.S.[69] It can be calculated from these statistics that the probability of alcoholism in a woman who has been married three times is almost four times greater than one who has been married only once. Since the "all women" figure (16 out of 100) includes the alcoholic women sample (45 out of 100) and roughly 10% of the population is addicted, when eliminating the alcoholic women, we find that less than 12% of non-alcoholic women have been married three times. Therefore, the likelihood is almost four times greater (45% to 12%). It would be higher, were it not for the fact that so many alcoholics die before having the opportunity to divorce and marry yet again. Up to 80% of all cases of divorce were attributable to alcoholism in the former Soviet Union, where alcoholism was (and still is) epidemic.[70]

The divorces are, in part, due to the alcoholic's propensity to create not only financial problems, but also engage in domestic violence and non-physical abuse. They may occur, as well, because of a greater tendency in addicts to commit adultery. Recovering alcoholic Conway Hunter, MD diplomatically points out, "Seeking companionship with members of the opposite sex outside of marriage is probably one of the most commonplace events that occurs in an alcoholic's life...."[71] Giving further support is the idea that when we have a relationship with a substance, there cannot be a close and significant one with another human being. Caroline Knapp points out that, in the extreme, anonymous sex gives "the illusion of intimacy with none of the attendant risks, none of the aching vulnerability of sober sex."[72]

8. Has serious problems at work

According to a report by the National Council on Alcohol and Drug Dependence, Inc. (NCADD), 85% of alcoholics and 70% of illegal drug addicts are employed.[73] The idea that these addicts are probably the cause of a disproportionate number of problems in the workplace is supported in the same paper. A year after employees identified as alcoholics at the Oldsmobile plant in Lansing, Michigan underwent treatment, grievances declined by 78% and disciplinary problems by 63%.[74] These are compelling statistics, considering the fact that many alcoholics may have gone undetected. Furthermore, most in treatment would still be in post-acute withdrawal, the early and difficult period of recovery in which many of the symptoms of active alcoholism often continue. According to relapse prevention experts Terence Gorski and Merlene Miller,[75] this period is effectively any period in-between drinks lasting up to 18 months and occasionally longer. The symptoms include an inability to think clearly, memory problems, emotional overreactions or numbness, sleep disturbances, physical coordination problems and stress sensitivity. Authors James Milam and Katherine Ketcham[76] report on much the same condition, referring to it as "protracted withdrawal syndrome." The alcoholic may continue "to be depressed, shaky, and irritable many days, months, or even years after his last drink, and [is the reason] why so many alcoholics return to drinking after a period of sobriety." Considering the behaviors exhibited in early recovery, the decline in grievances and disciplinary problems among recovering alcoholics with less than one year sober is astounding.

Other studies have shown those identified as having alcoholism were about one-third less productive than non-alcoholic (or, we might note, early-stage and, hence, undiagnosed alcoholic) employees.[77]

Except for those in seasonal or project-based businesses such as farming or film production, numerous changes in employment (often a sign of work-related problems) may be an excellent indicator of middle-stage alcoholism or poly-drug addiction.

9. Has recurring financial difficulties

There are numerous legitimate reasons for financial difficulties, just as there are for on-road accidents. Financial risk such as the decline of industries, unforeseen increases in interest rates, abrupt drops in asset values or the financial equivalent of "driver error", like potholes and fog, can lead to serious missteps. However, alcoholism increases the odds of slipping up. Conversely, *repeated* instances of overspending, carelessness in acquiring debt or loss of job/business may be a sign of poor judgment, the underlying cause of which is often alcoholism. Furthermore, the non-alcoholic often slows down at the first sign of financial "fog" and doesn't usually make the same financial mistake twice. Sober individuals are more likely to quickly correct and recover from such calamities than are middle-to-latter stage addicts. This is particularly true of debt and bank-ruptcy.

It's difficult to estimate the percentage of recurring financial troubles that may be linked to alcoholism. We don't have a National Highway Traffic Safety Administration study equivalent studying probabilities of financial misbehaviors due to this disease. However, a case could be made that we can extrapolate from the NHTSA study, linking DUIs and on-road behaviors to all other areas of life. The reckless abandon with which the early-stage alcoholic conducts himself on the road is probably similar in principle to the way in which he manages his financial affairs. The percentage of serious financial mishaps resulting from alcoholism may be similar to that of on-road crashes due to a combination of risk-taking behaviors and errors endemic to middle-stage addiction.

Anecdotally, I've found that the rate of alcoholism among those repeatedly mired in financial turbulence is far higher than in others. My best guess, based on experience as an Enrolled Agent and Certified Financial Planner™ licensee, is that 50% or so of bankruptcies can be directly linked to an alcohol or other drug addict. Bankruptcy attorneys knowledgeable in addiction concur, and agree that a large percentage of those remaining are likely vic-tims of addicts.[78] In addition, about half of those for whom I have prepared a series of delinquent tax returns have been alcohol and/or other drug addicts. Many of the other half, have been their victims. When one's life falls into dis-array, filing tax returns can be put on the back burner. I once asked an IRS agent specializing in late filing enforce-ment whether it had occurred to him that many of these extreme procrastinators were likely addicts. He responded, "We have found that these people's troubles seem to be far greater than the problems the IRS has in extracting a tax return from them."

10. Children are out-of-control

Having well-behaved children can be a way by which the addict inflates his ego. Many successful screen stars owe their start to an alcoholic parent or business manager who had an insatiable need to win at any cost, including having their own youngster forego childhood in exchange for the limelight. Brooke Shields, whose mother helped make her a star, may serve as one of the best-known examples. Patty Duke's alcoholic business managers pushed her into stardom, at great personal cost to Duke.

On the other hand, once the alcoholic parent is out of control, the children often follow suit. Researchers in Leningrad found that misbehaviors among children in the former Soviet Union were related to "problem" drinkers in either or both parents in 88 out of every 100 such families.[79] This should not be surprising, since the addict parent, for all intents and purposes, abandons the children in order to carry on a love affair with the drug. The child sees the private behavior in a parent and may even mimic it in his own way. A horrifying extreme example of this was the case of two boys, ages 10 and 11, who in 1994 dropped five-year-old Eric Morse from the 14th floor of a Chicago public housing complex because he wouldn't steal candy for them. Since the fathers of both boys were in prison, the probability of addiction in either was 80-90%. One of the mothers repeatedly missed school-counseling sessions, a behavior indicative of alcohol or other drug addiction. The other mother was a known drug addict.[80]

Another reason for a loss of control in children may be over-permissiveness by the alcoholic parent in an attempt to compensate for guilt about the behaviors and aftermath resulting from a drinking episode. Even if the alcoholic is incapable of remembering his actions in a light that is not self-favoring the results of such episodes may stare him in the face. Regardless of the reason, a lack of boundaries in children is a clear sign of possible alcoholism in one or more parents.

We may note that not all non-addict children growing up in even extremely dysfunctional situations spiral out of control. Authors Beth Polson and Newton Miller show that children react to the family addict by adopting different roles. Just as addicts vary in the manifestations of the disease, so do codependents in their reactions. Such roles are often not out-of-control behaviors. One style is distinguished by striving to offset the addict's poor conduct by becoming very controlled and even over-achieving. Another is characterized by attempts to defuse the family storm by performing or being cute and cuddly in an effort to get the family to laugh, while yet another withdraws physically and/or psychologically, hiding in his own fantasy world. Only one role is obviously destructive, imitating the misbehaviors in an effort to take the focus of attention off the addict. This is probably the type of non-addict most likely to be involved in criminal activities.[81]

11. Is careless of his or her family's welfare

Early-stage alcoholism is often hidden under a layer of competence. This is as true of home-life as for work. There is ego-gratification in developing one's abilities while committing emotional abuse in both the professional and personal areas of one's life.

As alcoholism progresses into the latter stages or when there is polydrug use, the addict needs to concentrate his efforts more on obtaining the drug than inflating his ego. The family's welfare may go by the wayside as a necessary by-product of procuring and protecting the drug as he loses control over his use. Or, the addict may be so "out of it" that she leaves her children unattended in a car on a hot summer day, ending tragically in death from heatstroke. An addict parent whose finances have collapsed may even move into an area with a bad element, making hard drugs easy to obtain by trading sex for drugs, which might then be shared with the children. Taking action when early-stage behavioral clues become obvious can prevent many of these tragedies. The question should be repeated: what are we waiting for?

8

Apparent Mental Confusion

1. Suffers from a short attention span

This may truly be what therapists refer to as "attention deficit hyperactivity disorder."[82] On the other hand, the extreme case is more likely addiction (or exacerbated by it), whether in the older latter-stage alcoholic or younger polydrug addict.

The person with late-stage alcoholism suffers tremendously when he stops drinking. According to Milam and Ketcham, "As soon as the blood alcohol level begins to descend, the brain cells, or neurons, become excited and agitated. The entire brain is affected, as the sensitive neurons send out highly disorganized and chaotic distress signals. The brain is, in a sense, short-circuiting, and the resulting pandemonium creates...profound mental confusion [and] memory defects...."[83]Any number of observable symptoms may result, including a short attention span and related confusion. Note that this may be at its worst in-between drinking episodes, or when the BAL is declining.

2. Has an inability to multi-task

This may be due to the mental confusion resulting from the cessation of drinking or a very high blood alcohol level relative to the progression of the disease. Even early-stage alcoholics can experience this when their BAL exceeds .24 per cent, even if most seem to control use in a way that allows them to remain highly functional (especially at BALs between .10 and .20 per cent). As the alcoholism progresses into the middle-stage, tolerance gradually decreases. Eventually, the afflicted may be unable to multi-task at relatively low BALs.

3. Is constantly misplacing or losing things

This may be a sign of having had a blackout. Other people may be blamed for misplacing items, or accused of stealing them. The addict may deny that the object was last in his possession, contrary to all evidence. Alcoholics have even been known to "misplace" their cars, unable to recall where they parked or even, how they got home.

4. Is often tardy or absent

The study at the Oldsmobile plant cited earlier found that after treating the employees identified as having alcoholism, overall man-hours lost declined by 49 per cent and leaves of absence by 56 per cent.[84] Other studies have found that absenteeism among alcoholics or "problem drinkers" is four to eight times greater than for employees not recognized as such and as much as 16 times greater among employees with alcohol *and* other drug related problems.[85] Yet, alcoholic Senator Joseph McCarthy "could 'belt a fifth,'...between midnight and five A.M., catch a couple hours sleep, and be at his office at eight or nine...."[86] Rock musician and admitted alcoholic Grace

Slick was known for her reliability and punctuality prior to her recovery.[87] The early-stage alcoholic may be an over-achiever, which could require getting to work every day and doing so on time.

On the other hand, absenteeism or tardiness may provide management their first clue to addiction. Such irresponsible conduct, including coming home at 3 a.m. or other "mysterious appearance," could give a spouse identical information. By this time, there are usually multiple clues to middle-to-latter stage addiction. If the other indications point only to early-stage alcoholism, tardiness or absenteeism could be accounted for by the god-like feeling of power over others afforded by arriving late, or not at all.

5. Engages in erratic behavior

At this stage, the behavior is not erratic in the sense of wielding power capriciously. It is erratic due to the effect of the chemicals on the brain, making the behaviors increasingly unpredictable and without rhyme or reason, even to the addict. Observers may use the terms "crazy" or "bizarre" to describe the person. Making sense of such people generally requires understanding alcoholism and, especially, polydrug addiction.

6. Appears to have a Personality Disorder or mental illness

These span early- to latter-stage alcohol and other drug addiction, but become most obvious as a result of poly-drug use or during middle-stage alcoholism and beyond.

Personality Disorders are the psychologists' way of making insurance pay for treatment, since it so often refuses to pay such costs for alcohol/other drug addiction. As alcoholism becomes covered by more insurance plans, it will be more frequently diagnosed. However, it will probably take a generation for therapists to accept the idea that few Personality Disorders exist independently of addiction. There's simply too much time, effort and money at stake, invested in one's prior education. When I explained my view that because alcoholism mimics virtually all of the Disorders the underlying problem is usually alcoholism, one therapist said to me, "you're suggesting that practically everything I learned to become a therapist is worthless." There are both special interests and psychological concerns in maintaining the status quo.

Yet, it is predictable that alcoholism often takes form as one or more of these Disorders. Addiction causes the practicing addict to engage in behaviors that violate his core values. This conflict between behaviors and values feeds on itself, leading to repeated violations. This subjects the person to intense stress, causing him to play "Survival Games" that look like Personality Disorders. Most alcoholics succumb to this, at least to some degree.

The Disorders that are mimicked vary by type of drug and the Psychological Type of the addict. There is also an interrelationship between an addict's Type and the drugs he chooses. In addition, the drug often determines which Disorder(s) the addict may appear to have. While the specifics are beyond the scope of this book, a brief overview and one detailed example will greatly assist the Alcohol and other Drug Addiction Recognition Expert, a designation that any serious reader of this work may strive to have conferred, in identifying likely addicts.[88]

The main Disorders, listed in the psychologists' manual entitled, *Diagnostic and Statistical Manual of Mental Disorders, Fourth Edition, or DSM-lV™*, are names most lay persons have heard.[89] These include Anti-Social

Personality Disorder, Obsessive-Compulsive Personality Disorder, Dissociative Identity Disorder (formerly known as Multiple Personality Disorder), Borderline Personality Disorder, Schizophrenia, Paranoid Personality Disorder, Bipolar Disorder (formerly known as Manic Depressive) and Narcissistic Personality Disorder. Many therapists attempt to treat these Disorders and not alcoholism. "Dual-diagnosis," in which a patient is diagnosed with alcoholism and one or more of the Disorders, is all the rage even among many chemical dependency counselors. When asked how he could know whether a true Disorder exists until the alcoholism is in remission, one such counselor admitted that he could not, but that insurance and government programs more often pay the costs of treating Disorders than of alcoholism. Another became visibly upset when asked how symptoms could be treated without dealing with the underlying cause.

Anti-Social Personality Disorder requires "a pervasive pattern of disregard for and violation of the rights of others."[90] *The 16th Edition of the Merck Manual* (another important text for psychologists) describes that persons having this Disorder "flout normal rules of social order. [They] are impulsive, irresponsible, amoral, and unable to forgo immediate gratification..."[91] This "the rules are not for me" attitude is one of the hallmarks of many alcoholics. The impulsiveness and inability to forgo immediate gratification hints at damage to the neo-cortex that has allowed the limbic system to take charge.

Recall the study referred to earlier, in which Terence T. Gorski administered the MMPI (the psychologists' tool for diagnosing Disorders) twice in early sobriety, 20 days apart. The fact that the percentage scoring as likely sociopaths plummeted from over 90% to less than 10% provides further support for the idea that alcoholism is often at the root of behaviors commonly believed to indicate the existence of Personality Disorders.

Behaviors manifesting as **Bipolar Disorder**, formerly known as manic-depression, may result from extended amphetamine or cocaine use followed by a period of abstinence, or depressant drug use. Numerous therapists having an interest in historical analysis have misdiagnosed Adolf Hitler as having been Bipolar. However, he was an amphetamine addict from 1936 on, and a barbiturate user during WW-ll. The grandiose scheme laid out in *Mein Kampf* indicates the possibility of barbiturate addiction long before this time, but his mood swings became far more extreme and behaviors much more erratic during the known period in which amphetamine-barbiturate use was combined.[92]

Actress Vivien Leigh was repeatedly diagnosed as bipolar even while she drank regularly and heavily. Heavy drinking also preceded Patty Duke's well-known Bipolar Disorder. By the age of 14, her alcoholic business managers were feeding her Bloody Marys. She later took Phenobarbital, Percodan, Thorazine, Stelazine, Valium, Seconal and other tranquilizers. In her twenties, she was often "hung over most of the day because I drank most of the night."[93]

Bipolar Disorder no doubt exists independently of alcoholism. However, it is frequently diagnosed either when it is a symptom or has been triggered by addiction. The same may be true for **Schizophrenia**. Perhaps the best-known Schizophrenic in recent times is mathematician John Nash, portrayed in the movie "A Beautiful Mind." The first Schizophrenic episode portrayed was one in which Nash was drinking heavily with his imaginary friend which, if true, is suggestive of a possibility that alcoholism triggered or exacerbated Nash's Schizophrenia. Support for the idea that what appears to be Schizophrenia may often be rooted in alcoholism can be found in the fact that, according to Anne Wilson Schaef, "when the term 'schizophrenia' was first coined, [the definition] included alcoholism."[94] In addition, the illness is usually first observed in the middle teens to late twenties, generally well after use of alcohol and other drugs has begun.[95] Alcoholism is rarely suspected since most doctors know so little about it and hardly anyone suspects it at such a young age.

This is not to suggest that Schizophrenia does not exist without alcoholism. On the other hand, as early as 1897 Henry Maudley, MD, found that "intemperance stands next to [hereditary influence] in the list of efficient causes" of insanity. Maudley based his opinion in part on the experience of an asylum for the mentally ill in the early 1870s. (Although some may consider the idea of citing a report this early in the history of behavioral science questionable, we would today be hard-pressed to repeat this unintentional study of a form of coerced abstinence.) During the second half of the year 1871, only 24 new male patients were admitted to this asylum, "whereas there were 47 and 73 in the preceding and succeeding half years. During the first quarter of the year 1873, there were 10, whereas they were 21 and 18 in the preceding and succeeding quarters....There was...a similar experience at the County prison, the production of crime as well as of insanity having diminished in a striking manner....The exceptional periods corresponded exactly with the last two 'strikes' in the coal and iron industries" in the county where the asylum and prison were located. It is suggested that "the decrease was undoubtedly due mainly to the fact that the labourers had no money to spend in drinking and in debauchery, that they were sober and temperate by compulsion, the direct result of which was that there was a marked decrease in the production of insanity and of crime." The results suggest that a huge percentage of mental illness has its origination in alcoholism.[96]

An essential feature of **Borderline Personality Disorder** is "a pervasive pattern of instability of interpersonal relationships, self-image, and affects, and marked impulsivity..." Personal relationships fall apart in the lives of alcoholics often long before work does. "Marked impulsivity" is the expected result from damage to the neo-cortex caused by a buildup of acetaldehyde in the brain. Some Personality Types use relationships to inflate their ego, resulting in "frantic efforts to avoid real or imagined abandonment,"[97] which is another indicator of Borderline. In fact, it is symptomatic of alcoholism in some. This may have been the case for Winona Ryder's character in the movie, "Girl, Interrupted," who in my opinion may have been misdiagnosed as having Borderline Personality Disorder and whose correct diagnosis may have been alcoholism.

Narcissism may provide the best example of a listing by the *DSM-IV* of behaviors that appear indistinguishable from those of the practicing alcoholic. A diagnosis of this Disorder requires five or more of the following attributes:

• A grandiose sense of self-importance
•A preoccupation with "fantasies of unlimited success, power, brilliance, beauty or ideal love"
• A belief that he is "special" and can only be understood by, or associate with, other such persons
• A need for "excessive admiration."
• "...a sense of entitlement, i.e., unreasonable expectations

of especially favorable treatment or automatic compliance with his or her expectations."
• "Is inter-personally exploitative, i.e., takes advantage of others to achieve his or her own ends."
• A lack of empathy
• Envious of others, or thinks that they are envious of him
• Displays arrogant and haughty attitudes toward others.[98]

All of these criteria are symptoms of alcoholism. Let's take them one at a time, referring to each in order:

1. This is, essentially, the definition of inflated ego used to describe the self-view of practicing alcoholics ("an inordinately large sense of self-importance").

2. Alcoholics often inform others of yet their latest and greatest scheme or conquest. (The four preoccupations listed happen to roughly equate to the preoccupation that might be expected of each of the four basic human Temperaments. Therefore, a person of any Personality Type as measured by the Myers-Briggs Type Indicator can appear to have Narcissism.)

3. A belief that one is this special requires a high-minded view of self-importance, or inflated ego.

4. Expectations of such admiration also relate to the alcoholic's excessively high opinion of self.

5. A sense of entitlement exemplifies the behavior of the god-like controlling alcoholic, particularly among those seeking political favoritism or power.

6. Addicts, always under the impression that they are more important than is anyone else, exploit others in order to inflate their egos.

7. When addicted, even those who are normally empathic will appear unconcerned with the needs of others. Recovering addicts inform us that they were the center of their universe, and of yours.

8. Envy, or unreasonable resentments, may be related to euphoric recall, which results in blaming everyone else for one's troubles. After all, the addict who does no wrong cannot be to blame for problems either in his life or in the lives of others. On the other hand, being on par with God in early-stage alcoholism may result in a belief that others are envious of him.

9. The practicing egomaniac addict regularly displays such an arrogant and haughty attitude.

Five out of nine criteria must be met for a diagnosis of Narcissism. However, meeting even one of these raise suspicions of alcoholism.

Many therapists argue that alcoholism results from Personality Disorders. However, tests from which we could infer that one might have alcoholism because of personality problems have generally been administered during the first few days of abstinence. When such tests were repeated after three months, 70-80% of what appeared to have been Personality Disorders during the first ten days of sobriety had disappeared.[99] Considering the fact that it takes two or three years for the brain to do most of its healing and for a sense of normalcy to return, we might predict an even greater rate of what some might think of as "spontaneous remission" from Personality Disorders as time goes on. Therefore, we need to place the larger probability of the explanation for bizarre behaviors on alcohol and/or other drugs, until proven wrong. If there is addiction (the greater probability), the addict cannot be helped therapeutically. Since recovering addicts often admit that in providing plenty of excuses for drinking the therapist was the biggest enabler, offering psychological counseling to an addict is a treatment worse than the disease.

On the other hand, even if we see numerous behavioral indications, there may not be substance addiction. The studies mentioned above suggest that in about one instance out of five in which many symptoms are apparent, there is a true Disorder and no alcoholism. However, the fact that a relative few having what appear to be Personality Disorders do not have alcoholism does not mean the behaviors are not linked to the disease. In many of these instances, the person under scrutiny is a child of an alcoholic. Therefore in the vast majority of cases, the underlying cause — whether alcoholism or codependency — continues untreated.

7. Has attempted suicide

Middle-stage alcoholism is punctuated with repeated bouts of attempts at sobriety. At some level, the addict realizes there is a problem. In addition, there are moments of clarity between drinking episodes that allow him to see his role. If nothing else, he may find it impossible to ignore the aftermath of yet the latest drinking and its cleanup. Some, who are very destructive during the drinking, become repentant when abstinent. Like James, the subject in the longitudinal study conducted by George E. Vaillant, they may become extremely depressed due to having engaged in what they view as "pathological" behavior.

Euphoric recall, memory repression and blackouts usually serve to prevent alcoholics from remembering too much of their bad behaviors at one time. It may be that they are protected from this for good reason, since addicts can, as Vernon Johnson explained, go into "irreversible emotional shock" from remembering too much. Perhaps, this reduces the likelihood of suicide.

On the other hand, sometimes this protective mechanism fails, probably most often in early recovery or during short periods of abstinence from middle- to latter-stage alcoholism. The movie, "A Star is Born," portrayed such a situation. Failing actor Norman Maine, played by Fredric March in the 1937 version, was one of the class of 15% of alcoholics who lose their jobs, as work begins to interfere with drinking. When his wife, actress Esther Blodgett (played by Janet Gaynor) wins the Academy Award® for best actress, Maine climbs onto the stage uninvited and gives a vitriolic speech on winning the "worst actor" award. He's obviously long past the ego-inflating stage of alcoholism and well onto the path of self-destruction. Upon overhearing a conversation between Blodgett and a film director in which she proposes giving up her life as an actress so that she "can give Norman back his," Maine, grief-stricken and feeling totally inadequate, commits suicide.

Since alcoholics consist of about 10% of the population, it is significant that numerous studies report that alcoholics commit 20-30% of all suicides. However, these statistics appear to be missing many of the alcoholic-related suicides, which are euphemized into "other problems" the victim was having at the time, or those occurring in early sobriety. Some evidence for this can be derived from a study reported by the National Institute of Alcohol Abuse and Alcoholism.[100] The suicide rate for women in one year was about 9 per 100,000, while the rate for female alcoholics was 207 per 100,000, or 23 times greater. The mathematics of this suggests that 70% of all suicides among women may be connected to alcoholism.[101] Another study reporting the suicide rate among young Eskimos males at 25 times the national average also supports this estimate, since such males suffer a rate of alcoholism as high as 95% in some villages.[102]Another fact suggesting that the 20-30% rate is underreported is that even many middle-stage alcoholics go undiagnosed. In addition, the statistics appear not to include other substance addicts. Many polydrug addicts have entered rehab unaware of their addiction to alcohol, while countless observers had no idea there was an addiction to any drug. Consider the case of Elizabeth Taylor and ask, how many others knew of her condition prior to 1983?

"Maybe if someone had kicked me out [of my home] while I was drinking, I wouldn't have spent 20 years inside a bottle."
                    Detective Lennie Briscoe, "Law and Order"

9

Middle-to-Latter Stage Physical Signs

1. Has a poor diet

Some latter-stage alcoholics rarely eat, due to all the empty calories they take in from drinking. Many poly-drug addicts consume a fast-food diet of chips and other empty carbohydrates, in an attempt to increase blood sugar levels. According to alcoholism experts Milam and Ketcham, "the great majority of alcoholics suffer from chronic low blood sugar. When given the 5-hour glucose tolerance test, over 95 percent of both early- and late-stage alcoholics experience a spike in blood sugar level after intake of sugar and then a rapid plunge....Low blood sugar causes a craving for substances such as alcohol and sweets which can quickly raise the blood sugar and relieve the symptoms."[103] Gorski estimates that 40% of all alcoholics have hypoglycemia.[104]

Other drugs may also cause large swings in these levels. Stimulants cause the adrenal glands to produce epinephrine, which in turn stimulates the pancreas to secrete insulin, lowering blood-sugar levels. This doesn't explain why amphetamine addicts often eat little or nothing for extended periods, but could explain their extraordinary irritability.

On the other hand, it may be difficult to distinguish between non-addicts with severe hypoglycemia and alcoholics. The behavioral symptoms of low blood sugar include irritability, fatigue, stress and mental confusion, all indicative of alcoholism. Depression, agitation and erratic behavior are additional symptoms of low blood sugar. Depression includes whining and "crying the blues," which can easily lead to "blaming others." Agitation includes excitability, impatience, irritability, nervousness and tantrums. Erratic behavior includes acting irrationally, blackouts, confusion, delusion, memory lapses, an inability to concentrate and violent outbursts. These behaviors appear suspiciously similar to those of addicts.

It's likely that many of the most violent alcoholics are those with hypoglycemia. The combined effect could account for the fact that only 13 apprehended delinquents out of 129 in one study had normal blood sugar levels.[105] The recovering alcoholic bingeing on sweets and other simple or refined carbohydrates could help to explain the "dry drunk" syndrome, in which many of the alcoholic's bad behaviors resume during a subsequent sugar crash. Since this can lead to a quart of vodka instead of a gallon of ice cream, recovering addicts may find that an improvement in diet can help increase the odds of staying sober.

2. There is drug paraphernalia (whether or not "a friend's")

This is an excellent clue for parents of suspected polydrug addicts. Many household items can be used as paraphernalia, any one of which would generally raise no suspicions while several in conjunction should. These include roughly 6-inch paper squares, small balloons (filled with something or not), large or unusual-looking spoons, Q-Tips, razor blade(s), lighter(s), metal wire, coin-sized bags or cellophane baggies, artificial sweetener, tin foil and small pieces of folded newspaper containing baking soda. If these are found, consideration may be given to taking the items to authorities for testing of heroin, amphetamines, cocaine and other drugs.

3. Suffers from numerous illnesses at middle age

The Lansing, Michigan Oldsmobile plant study cited earlier found a 29% reduction in health care benefits used after treating alcoholic employees.[106] Another study showed addicts incurring 300% higher medical costs than non-addicts.[107] Anecdotal estimates on the percentage of hospital resources consumed by alcoholics are in the range of 50% and as high as 90% in some trauma wards.

Hundreds of secondary diseases and disorders are related to poor diet in latter-stage alcoholism. These include pneumonia, hepatitis, diabetes, cirrhosis, jaundice and ulcers (common even in earlier-stage alcoholics due to increased secretions of hydrochloric acid).[108]

Alcohol damages the small intestine, where many enzymes are formed to aid in digestion. With fewer enzymes, excessive amounts of food enter the colon undigested, causing gaseous distention and fermentation, resulting in diarrhea.

Since alcohol damages the liver, which is responsible for cleansing the body of carcinogens and regulating cholesterol, alcoholism frequently instigates or exacerbates cancer and heart disease.[109] Alcoholism also directly damages the heart, often leading to heart failure.[110] Pancreatitis often develops after a number of years of heavy drinking. An estimated 65% of pancreatic cancer can be linked to alcoholism.

Early death is indicative of alcoholism but, since by then it's too late, we might look to life-threatening illnesses as an indicator. The median age of death among women was in the 70s during most of the 20th century. Yet, the median age of death among famous female alcoholics, according to statistics culled from Lucy Barry Robe's study, was barely over 50 during the same period, with over two-thirds having died by age 62.

On the other hand, some alcoholics feign illness in order to obtain more drugs. They may exaggerate concern over their children's health in order to obtain drugs for themselves in their child's name. "Sneaky" may not be a strong enough word to describe the behaviors in which many alcoholics engage.

4. Has serious illnesses at a young age

The young poly-drug addict often experiences repeated colds, viruses and bronchitis.[111] Due to the sense of invincibility resulting from early-stage alcoholism, multiple sex partners and unprotected sex are common. The "politically correct" crusade protecting gays from being profiled has prevented the dissemination of the idea that substance addiction is at the root of much unprotected sex in many areas, resulting in far more cases of AIDS than there would otherwise be. Yet, anecdotes among both male and female homosexuals suggest heavy drug use among those engaging in unsafe sex with large numbers of partners. Since such use can be connected to a sense of invincibility, addiction is likely. Further evidence supporting a link between alcoholism and sexually-transmitted diseases can be found in the former Soviet Union, where up to 90% of syphilis and 95% of gonorrhea cases were found to be associated with alcohol "abuse."[112]

5. Sleeps on the job

Few early-stage alcoholics, driven by the need to inflate the ego, falter on the job. On the other hand, those addicts specializing, so to speak, in amphetamines, experience "crashes" after being up for days on speed. Middle- to latter-stage alcoholics experience increasing physical problems, which can translate to sleeping at inappropriate times. Recovering ex-cons report that such sleeping is common among prison guards.

6. Pupils are dilated or constricted

Pupil dilation and constriction are clues to stimulant or opiate use. Pupils are usually one-quarter to one-half the size of the iris, depending on lighting. Anything smaller, especially if pinpoint, is indicative of opiate (heroin, morphine) or synthetic opiate (Vicodin, Oxycontin, codeine) use in non-therapeutic doses. Anything larger, especially in adults, is an almost-certain sign of non-caffeine stimulant use.

7. Has a "glassy eyes" look

If you look carefully, you'll see that Marilyn Monroe's eyes were glassy in her later movies. While such eyes can be sensuous, they were a result of drinking vodka on the set, which isn't very sexy when we consider the implications. Glassy eyes were the only signs of a high blood alcohol level evident in Henri Paul, which could be seen in the hotel video prior to the Princess Diana tragedy.

8. Eyes are red, glazed or tired-looking

"The eyes tell all," is very true in regards to addiction. Aside from dilation, constriction and the glassy look, red eyes are a result of heavy alcohol use in some and marijuana use in many. Due to lack of sleep, stimulants can result in a glazed or tired look.

9. Has a puffy face, heavy bags under the eyes, showing signs of premature aging or reddening of the facial skin

When combined, alcoholism, smoking and sun are lethal for the skin. As with every clue viewed in isolation, there may be other causes, in this case premature wrinkling. However, as is true for other clues, symptoms must be considered in conjunction with one another.

Puffiness in the face is common in latter-stage alcoholics, due to the build-up of fatty deposits resulting from a lifetime of heavy alcohol use. Bags under the eyes, too, are indicative of alcoholism. When observed with erratic behaviors, we can ascribe a very high likelihood of this affliction.

10. Has "rules" for using

Many recovering alcoholics tell us that they never felt they had alcoholism because they didn't drink on weekdays, or before 7pm, or 6pm, or 5pm, or noon. They'd stick to their "rules" until broken and would then make less stringent rules or eliminate them completely after years of slow erosion.

Others set rules for type of drink. Since 1 1/2 ounces of 80-proof liquor contains the same alcohol as 5 ounces of wine or 12 ounces of beer, many drink only wine or beer in a desperate attempt to keep the alcohol intake down. "I'm no alcoholic; I don't drink that hard stuff," is a common refrain among practicing alcoholics. Unfortunately, there are plenty of winos. Two bottles of wine over a 12-hour period will result in a blood alcohol level of .18 per cent for a 120 pound person, as will three bottles for a 200 pound person.

At one upper-class treatment facility for alcoholics, 15% of the patients never drank anything but beer during their entire drinking careers.[113] The 200 pound person needs only two 6-packs of beer over four hours or three in 12 hours to bring his blood alcohol level to .18 per cent. Recall that once at this level, maintenance requires only three-quarters of a beer — a mere 9 ounces — every hour.

Other rules for use include never drinking alone ("people who drink alone are alcoholics!") and never drinking before driving with their kids in the car. One of the fundamental distinctions between addicts and non-addicts regarding their drinking behavior is that non-addicts don't need to create strict rules regarding drinking, because when, what or how much they drink is not an issue. Alcoholics break rules and continuously create new ones. By the time these rules become evident, the observer may witness a "preoccupation with the drug," a result of "impaired control over drinking." This generally occurs only after a tremendous amount of damage has already been done.

11. "Hangs out" with obvious addicts (lower companions)

Many alcoholics push others into drinking or using. However, it's easier if he doesn't have to push, accounting for the fact that most alcoholics have "drinking buddies." This also makes it easy for him to rationalize that he drinks no more than the average Joe or that "Joe" drinks so much that *he* must be an alcoholic. This also puts the focus on someone else's drinking rather than his own, serving as a sort of "cover" for his own use. Alcoholics also find other addicts who are more troubled and irresponsible than are they, who can be controlled in an effort to prop up what is by now a faltering ego. They are prolific at identifying others who may have alcoholism, but never themselves until in recovery, even though addicts are all around them.

This can be a very useful clue for identifying adolescent polydrug addicts. Many kids don't "get in with bad kids and then start using drugs," as is commonly believed. Addicts usually slip into addiction without anyone being the wiser, at a very young age. Most young addicts *seek out* other addict kids after having triggered the disease, usually with alcohol. Barely one adult in a thousand would suspect that the initial use of this legal drug set off illegal drug addiction in their child.

12. Takes extreme measures to insure that the substance is always available

This goes beyond "partying." At this stage, the drug must, quite simply, be available, hidden or not. The latter-stage addict will go to any lengths to insure such availability. At this point, his brain's ability to produce neurotransmitters is greatly diminished. He needs the substance just to "normalize," as Nicholas Cage's character did in the movie "Leaving Las Vegas," and Ray Milland's in "Lost Weekend." As previously pointed out, when the alcoholic at this stage stops drinking, "all hell breaks loose." He must continue drinking or using at all costs.

13. Hides the odor

Alcoholics are known to reek not of alcohol, but instead of perfume, cologne, gum or mouthwash. At this stage, they are, in effect, engaged in a game of hiding the liquor, usually symptomatic of middle- to latter-stage alcoholism.

Many female alcoholics are poly-drug addicts and have become so early on in an effort to continue to appear "lady-like." Making sure they don't smell like whiskey, they learn to mix alcohol with pills. Many other drugs bind to the same neurotransmitter receptors that alcohol does, but in a non-competitive way: they bind to different sites on the same receptors.[114] This results in potentiation, in which the effect of one drink combined with one pill may equal an enhanced effect of as much as six to eight drinks. Alcoholism expert Stanley E. Gitlow, MD, coined the term "sedativism" to describe the cross addiction to alcohol and other sedative-hypnotic drugs. Gitlow believed that half of alcoholic women might have had sedativism as early as 1980, when he also felt that two-thirds of women under age 30 were afflicted with this disease. In 1983, Betty Ford said that 80% of female addicts combined alcohol with either sedative-hypnotics or synthetic opiates.[115]

14. Pulls a "geographic" (suddenly moves or does so numerous times)

Some early-stage alcoholics move often. This may be to switch identities, in a sense, since they have often ruined the lives of others, or to inflate their ego with an additional dose of stress and excitement in their lives. More often, those in the latter stages frequently move in what usually turns out to be a vain attempt to improve their situation or effect a "geographic cure." Unfortunately, as recovering alcoholics themselves put it, they bring the drunk with them. One well-known alcoholic, Ludwig van Beethoven, reportedly changed his residence 71 times in 35 years.[116] He was also a promiscuous womanizer, reminiscent of the dreams of another blind (even if fictional) alcoholic, Lt. Col. Frank Slade.

15. Hides the liquor

This is the classic sign that codependents look for to confirm a diagnosis of alcoholism. Unfortunately, it is long after most of the other-destructive behaviors in the life of the alcoholic have occurred, when he is on the path towards self-destruction.

The secret places famous people have hidden their drugs of choice are legendary. Judy Garland's third husband, Sid Luft, found "small envelopes of Seconal and Benzedrine hidden everywhere: Scotch-taped inside the drapes...under the carpets...[in the] bedsprings; in the lining of Judy's terrycloth bathrobe; tablets and capsules buried deep inside her bath powder and secreted under her books."[117] Less famous addicts, when in recovery, have told stories of alcohol strapped to the underside of cars, in toilet tanks, inside dust bags of vacuum cleaners, in the kitchen cabinets disguised in vinegar bottles or in the bathroom medicine cabinet inside bottles of eye solution or Listerine. More than one recovering alcoholic has told how he would fill the windshield wiper fluid compartment of his car with rum and run the wiper tubes through a hole in the dash. He could be seen sipping a little Coke when driving. After hitting the wiper fluid button to clean already squeaky-clean windows, voila! Instant rum and Coke. Anyone who hides his drug in such creative ways is, very clearly, an addict. He is likely in the latter stages since, by this time, others have made the connection between poor conduct and use, and because he cannot be without his drug.

"Maybe if someone had kicked me out [of my home] while I was drinking, I wouldn't have spent 20 years inside a bottle."
                            Detective Lennie Briscoe, "Law and Order"

10

So What Do You Do?

Now that you realize a number of persons in your life, past or present, have alcoholism, what do you do? As for those in the past, my sincere hope is that you are able to heal by understanding alcoholism. Consider the fact that however painful the experience, you survived. It could have been worse.

You now have the tools to quickly identify likely addicts and protect yourself. Anything you can do to assist them in experiencing consequences should be considered, but be wary of being dragged into something that could be financially and emotionally grueling. You need to stay healthy before considering crusades from which you could find it difficult to extricate yourself. A desire to get and stay sober is a rare event in the life of an alcoholic. Why should he? His biochemistry impels him to drink and he is incapable of seeing that any problems result from the use of the drug. Further, the ego satisfaction derived from success at school, work, play and/or crime, so common to early-stage alcoholism, helps to insure that perceived benefits from use exceed costs for years and, often, decades.

If involved in a personal or professional relationship

with a practicing alcoholic, disengaging and administering uncompromising tough love is essential. Countless victims admit they had no idea that the addict in their life was capable of committing horrible deeds. Recovering alcoholics are clear about the need for pain to inspire them to get sober. Severe consequences are usually the best hope to regain a person who, underneath the wreckage of addiction, may be kind-hearted, loving, honest and competent. However, we're human. We find it difficult, as non-addicts or recovering alcoholics, to administer pain, even when logically, we know that pain is the addict's best friend. Further, once you stop enabling, there is almost always someone else to take your place. This requires that other close persons also understand addiction and stop protecting the addict from his own misbehaviors.

Because of the difficulty in watching someone suffer and in creating a united front, the legal system should be used whenever possible to require abstinence. Unfortunately, the system needs dramatic improvement. Too many law enforcers are themselves alcoholics, which not only sets a poor example, but also can help to create injustice. The courts don't forge the connection between the use of the drug and the misbehaviors in which the person has engaged; unless illegal drugs are involved, they rarely even require treatment. A system that fails to treat the cause and addresses only symptoms is one relegated to serving as a turnstile.

All-too-often, tragedy occurs with few having even an inkling of the extent of the problem. Rob Waldron's story in "Newsweek" on his brother, Ryan, is typical.[118] Ryan, a senior in college, was killed in an alcohol-related crash that was reported by officers to be among the worst they had ever seen. It was only after his death that Ryan's family realized that he had "developed a drinking problem." They were unaware of the fact that "he drank to excess at nearly every social function, usually three to four times a week."

Often, even when the extent of the problem is known, the family is unwilling or unable to intervene appropriately. Because they don't understand alcoholism, they think of it as a "rite of passage," or something over which self-control will be learned. Official sanctions can take the place of intervention and may, if there are family members who "don't get it," even be more effective. If a student exhibits signs of alcoholism, he can be threatened with expulsion if he doesn't regularly and randomly test clean and sober. In the same way, a driver found guilty of DUI can be required to submit to regular blood and urine tests as a condition of retaining his license. If he fails, he loses his license. If he drives without a license, society has the right to take much stronger action, including sending him to prison. Many recovering alcoholics report that a credible threat of a loss of an important privilege forced them into a program of sobriety.

Most alcoholics engage only periodically in behaviors that provide what seems a valid reason to intervene. Many regularly disparage others, but even though often a terrific clue to alcoholism, this is probably not a behavior over which one can successfully require abstinence. Some commit domestic violence, but usually not often. They generally don't steal, embezzle or even lie in a way that could cause serious harm to others, with regularity. However, the typical alcoholic does engage in one potentially lethal behavior an estimated 80 times per year: he drinks beyond the legal limit and gets behind the wheel of a motor vehicle. And, as we discovered earlier, he is hardly ever apprehended.

The DUI is the one repeated violation for which we often have a solid reason to intervene. Further, it generally proves the connection between use and misbehaviors, and provides justification to enforce abstinence through legal sanctions. Yet, this most effective intervention is rarely used. On those rare occasions when apprehended, the violator is required to attend DUI school. We think he can "learn" to not drink and drive. We impose costs and require abstinence while driving, yet we don't impose the most logical and appropriate consequence of all: no use allowed, period. Almost every alcoholic who periodically drinks and drives says he'll never do it again. He truly means it, when he's sober. Yet, when he begins drinking, biochemistry takes over. He experiences feedback that causes him to believe he is on par with God. Of course he can drive—he can do anything.

We declare war on drugs and, in prison, pruno, a foul-tasting alcohol that inmates make from canned fruit. We think that by prohibiting drugs, addicts will get clean. Yet, the best hope is to test for the drug with a guarantee of consequences for failure. Anyone who proves by his behavior that he cannot drink or use safely, i.e., without acting destructively, should be offered a choice of abstinence or consequences. In our private lives, we can give likely alcoholics the choice of sobriety or termination of a relationship, whether romantic or professional. In the public sphere, we might require abstinence as a condition of retaining one's license, remaining on parole or earning an early release from prison. Many use drugs for social and religious functions, medical needs, even recreation, without acting destructively. Therefore, focusing on the person rather than the drug is appropriate in a free society. We need to admit that the problem is not the drug, but rather the person on the drug. The political system must narrow the focus of this war if we are to have any hope of solving the problem. This requires that abstinence be coerced only in those whose conduct proves they cannot use without violating the rights of others.

Taking advantage of the opportunities to intervene in the lives of addicts won't help with those who have already become the Joseph Stalin's, Adolf Hitler's, Jeffrey Dahmer's and Saddam Hussein's of the world. However, coercing abstinence can do a lot to make the world safer and far more rewarding in our everyday lives. It might even prevent the next Stalin or other tyrant from coming to power. But we must first overcome the fear of diagnosing addiction. Alcoholism should not be a stigma; it is an explanation for most misbehavior, and an extraordinarily accurate predictor of uncivilized conduct. We need to begin acting early rather than stalling, hoping that "it will get better," or, "she'll grow out of it," or, "we can talk to him." If it's alcoholism, it won't, she won't, and no you can't. Delay only increases the odds of tragedy. I'll ask again: what are we waiting for?

Appendix I
New Thorburn Substance Addiction Recognition Indicator

Scoring: Score each clue on a scale of zero to five, with zero being no problem at all of which you are aware and five being a definite serious problem. Before scoring, read the section that describes the indication.

Early-Stage Indicators
Ego Inflating Factors
(Supreme Being and Sense of Invincibility)

Score (0 - 5)
1. Over-achieves, at any cost
2. Regularly uses foul language
3. Smokes
4. Extraordinarily charming (manipulates)
5. Occupation allows wielding of power
6. Occupation allows ease of use
7. Engages in risky behaviors in reckless fashion
8. Has a "the rules don't apply to me" attitude
9. Compulsive gambler
10. Compulsive spender/other compulsions affecting ability to function
11. Pontificates (dogmatic and arrogant)
12. Uses twisted logic

13. Is a great liar
14. Repeatedly makes unkept promises
15. Belittles and disparages others
16. Gets others to play the "blame game"
17. Has ever knowingly made a false accusation
18. Wields power capriciously
19. Has knowingly betrayed another
20. Has a need to win at any cost
21. Has serious problems at home
22. Intimidates others to get his way
23. Engages in "telephonitis"
24. Repeatedly hangs up abruptly on others
25. Engages in serial Don Juanism or adultery
26. Hates others
27. Verbally abuses others
28. Physically abuses others
29. Has engaged in reprenhesible, even if legal, behaviors
30. Engages in unnecessarily reckless behaviors
31. Has recently had an accident, especially several
32. Drives while under the influence
33. Has committed a felony
34. Is of high risk ethnic background
35. Has close relatives with alcoholism
36. Drinks champagne or mixes liquor with soda
37. Drinks heavily on an empty stomach
38. Seems to always be having "a party" or going to one
39. Gulps or "chugs" alcohol
40. Does not appear inebriated at .10 to .20 BAL

Add up the score

Question #	Score (0-5)	Question #	Score (0-5)
1		21	
2		22	
3		23	
4		24	
5		25	
6		26	
7		27	
8		28	
9		29	
10		30	
11		31	
12		32	
13		33	
14		34	
15		35	
16		36	
17		37	
18		38	
19		39	
20		40	

Sub-total _____   _____

Grand Total └_____> _____

A score of 0-25 indicates a normal human who makes an average number of life mistakes. If you know the person well who you score within this range, the probability of alcoholism is remote, although not unheard of. However, if you don't yet know the person or are just getting to know him/her and there is a score of even 10, caution should be exercised in dealings and your antennae should be up.

A score of 25-50 suggests a potential problem. He or she may have alcoholism and is struggling with it, attempting to make up for bad behaviors when between drinking episodes. Alternatively, s/he may be a codependent to someone who has a serious problem.

A score of 50-200 suggests a high probability of early-stage alcoholism. This person should be treated as extremely dangerous to your physical, psychological/emotional and/or financial well being.

Middle-to-Latter Stage Indicators of Alcoholism or Polydrug Addiction
(Poor Judgment or Signs of Apparent Mental Confusion)

Scoring: Score each clue on a scale of zero to five, with zero being no problem at all of which you are aware and five being a definite serious problem. Before scoring, read the section that describes the indication.

Score (0 - 5)

1. Under-achiever
2. Plays the "blame game"
3. Has unreasonable resentments
4. Makes repeated promises to "never do it again"
5. Has a poor personal or professional reputation
6. Has very loose sexual morals
7. Has been married/divorced several times
8. Has serious problems at work

9. Experiences recurring financial difficulties
10. Children are out-of-control
11. Is careless of his family's welfare
12. Exhibits a short attention span
13. Has an inability to multi-task
14. Frequently misplaces or loses things
15. Is often tardy or absent
16. Engages in erratic behavior (appears "crazy")
17. Appears to be Sociopathic
18. Appears to be manic-depressive (Bipolar)
19. Appears to be Schizophrenic
20. Appears to be Narcissistic
21. Appears to have another Personality Disorder
22. Has attempted suicide
23. Has a poor diet
24. You find drug paraphernalia
25. Has suffered numerous illnesses in middle age
26. Has suffered serious illness at a young age
27. Sleeps on the job or other inappropriate times
28. Pupils are dilated or constricted
29. Has a "glassy eyes" look
30. Eyes are red, glazed or tired
31. Has a puffy face ("chipmunk" look)
32. Has heavy bags under the eyes
33. Suffers from premature aging
34. Has "rules" for use
35. Hangs out with obvious addicts
36. Takes extreme measures to insure availability
37. Attempts to hide the odor
38. Pulls a "geographic" (may "suddenly" move)
39. Moves numerous times lacking good cause
40. Hides the liquor

Add up the score

Question #	Score (0-5)	Question #	Score (0-5)
1		21	
2		22	
3		23	
4		24	
5		25	
6		26	
7		27	
8		28	
9		29	
10		30	
11		31	
12		32	
13		33	
14		34	
15		35	
16		36	
17		37	
18		38	
19		39	
20		40	

Sub-total _____   _____

Grand Total ⌐————————————→ _____

A score of 0-25 indicates a normal human who makes an average number of life mistakes. If you know the person well and the score is within this range, the probability of alcoholism is remote, unless the early-stage score is high or would have been high earlier in his or her life. There is also a possibility of serious codependency. If you don't yet know the person or are just getting to know him/her and there is a score of even 10, caution should be exercised in dealings and your antennae should be up.

A score of 25-50 suggests a potential problem. He or she may have middle-to-latter stage alcoholism or polydrug addiction and is struggling with it, attempting to make up for bad behaviors when between drinking episodes.

A score of 50-200 suggests a high probability of middle-stage alcoholism or worse. This person should be treated as extremely dangerous to your physical, psychological/emotional and/or financial well being.

Appendix II
Alcohol Takes a Shotgun Approach;
Other Drugs are Laser-Like

	Disables Glutamate	Increases GABA	Boosts Dopamine	Releases Endorphins	Boosts Seratonin
Alcohol	X	X	X	X	X
Sedatives	X				
Valium		X			
Cocaine			X		
Heroin				X	

Appendix III

Resources

Al-Anon
www.al-anon.org

Alcoholics Anonymous
www.aa.org

American Council for Drug Education
www.acde.org

Children of Alcoholics Foundation
www.coaf.org

International Council for Addiction Studies Research
www.incase.org

Join Together
National Resource for Communities fighting substance abuse.
www.jointogether.org

Narcotics Anonymous
www.na.org

National Association of Addiction Treatment Providers
www.naatp.org

National Council on Alcohol and Drug Dependence
www.ncadd.org

PrevenTragedy Foundation
A non-profit organization that is dedicated to promulgating the idea that early identification of alcoholism helps prevent tragedy.
www.PrevenTragedy.org.

The Phoenix House Foundation
www.phoenixhouse.com

Sober House
Housing for those in early sobriety.
www.soberhouse.com

Sober Recovery
Resource directory.
www.soberrcovery.com

Endnotes

1. Lester Grinspooon, MD and James B. Bakalar, JD, "Mental Health Review," President and Fellows of Harvard College, 1990, p. 6. The study is reported in George E. Vaillant, *The Natural History of Alcoholism Revisited*, Cambridge, MA: Harvard University Press, 1995, pp. 104-108.

2. Martha Morrison, *White Rabbit: A Doctor's Story of Her Addiction and Recovery*, New York: Crown Publishers, 1989, pp. 49, 109-111 and 119.

3. The biology is from Dr. James R. Milam and Katherine Ketcham, *Under the Influence: A Guide to the Myths and Realities of Alcoholism*, New York: Bantam Books, 1983, pp. 35-39. However, the interpretation is mine.

4. I make a case for 80% in Doug Thorburn, *Drunks, Drugs & Debits: How to Recognize Addicts and Avoid Financial Abuse*, Northridge, CA: Galt Publishing, 2000, pp. 14-15. However, most recovering addict ex-cons interviewed since suggest that the percentage is well over 90%.

5. Vernon Johnson, *I'll Quit Tomorrow*, San Francisco, CA: Harper and Row, 1980.

6. S.I. Hayakawa, *Language in Thought and Action*, Harcourt, Brace and Company: New York, 1949.

7. Particularly his Jungian or Myers-Briggs Personality Type.

8. See Appendix II, "Alcohol Takes a Shotgun Approach; Other Drugs are Laser-Like."

9. Sally Ann Berk, *The Martini Book*, NY: Black Dog & Leventhal Publishers, p. 73.

10. Harry M. Tiebout, MD, "The Ego Factors in Surrender to Alcoholism," New Brunswick, NJ: Journal of Studies on Alcohol, Inc., Vol. 15, pp. 610-621.

11. Thorburn, Ibid.

12. James Graham, *The Secret History of Alcoholism: The Story of Famous Alcoholics and Their Destructive Behavior*, Rockport, MA: Element Books, 1996.

13. Lucy Barry Robe, *Co-Starring Famous Women and Alcohol: the dramatic truth behind the tragedies and triumphs of 200 celebrities*, Minneapolis, MN: CompCare Publications, 1986, pp. 47-48.

14. Graham, Ibid., and Donald W. Goodwin, MD, *Alcoholism and the Writer*, Kansas City: Andrews and McMeel, 1988, quoted in Graham, Ibid., pp. 8-9. In 1993, Toni Morrison, in whom I have no evidence of alcoholism, made it five out of eight.

15. Milam and Ketcham, Ibid.

16. James E. Royce and David Scratchley, *Alcoholism and Other Drug Problems*, New York: The Free Press, 1996, p. 176.

17. Robe, Ibid., p. 287.

18. National Council on Alcoholism and Drug Dependence, Inc., "Fact Sheet: Alcoholism and Alcohol Related Problems," 12 West 221 Street, New York, NY 10010, May, 1995.

19. Father Joseph C. Martin, *Chalk Talks on Alcohol*, San Francisco, CA: Harper and Row, 1989, p. 73.

20. Thorburn, Ibid., pp. 333-334.

21. Los Angeles Daily News, "Toll evader denies everything," November 26, 2000.

22. Terence T. Gorski and Merlene Miller, *Staying Sober: A Guide for Relapse Prevention*, Independence, MO: Herald House/Independence Press, 1986, p. 120.

23. From a conversation with Brubaker, a therapist in Casa Grande, Arizona. Mike Brubaker, with Ken Estes, wrote *Deadly Odds: Recovery From Compulsive Gambling*, New York: Simon and Schuster, Fireside/Parkside Books, 1994.

24. Gorski and Miller, Ibid., p. 124

25. Donald H. Dunn, *Ponzi! The Boston Swindler*, New York: McGraw-Hill Book Company, 1975, p. 179.

26. Ibid. p. vii; italics in the original.

27. Ibid., p. 253.

28. Graham, Ibid., pp. 114-115.

29. Ibid., pp. 122-125.

30. Arts and Entertainment Network, "Ku Klux Klan: A Secret History," aired on September 26, 1999.

31. Graham, Ibid., made this point.

32. Paul and Shirley Eberle, *The Abuse of Innocence: The McMartin Preschool Trial*, Buffalo, New York: Prometheus Books, 1993, pp. 34 and 46.

33. Quoted in Graham, Ibid., p. 12.

34. Graham, Ibid., p. 37.

35. Ibid., pp. 37-50.

36. On the other hand, Hanssen's father, who was verbally and physically abusive toward Robert, may have been the alcoholic behind his son's behavior. The same may be true of Benedict Arnold, whose father was a known alcoholic.

37. B. D. Hyman, *My Mother's Keeper: A daughter's candid portrait of her famous mother*, New York: William Morrow and Co., 1985.

38. Thorburn, Ibid., pp. 166-170.

39. *Macbeth*, Act II, Scene 3, line 34.

40. "Eldridge Cleaver's Last Gift: the Truth," David Horowitz, The Los Angeles Times, May 3, 1998.

41. Dan Carter, *The Politics of Rage*, New York: Simon & Schuster, 1995, p. 104.

42. Marshall Frady, *Wallace*, New York: Random House, 1996, p. 81.

43. Maria Roy, Ed., *Battered Women: A Psychosociological Study of Domestic Violence*, New York: Van Nostrand, 1977.

44. Ibid., p. 39.

45. Neil Jacobson and John Gottman of the University of Washington, and other studies interpreted by Margaret A. Hagen in, "Bad Attitude," National Review, July 20, 1998, p. 38.

46. Graham, Ibid.; Leonard L. Heston, MD and Renate Heston, R.N., *The Medical Casebook of Adolf Hitler*, New York: Stein and Day, 1980; Dr. Li Zhisui, *The Private Life of Chairman Mao*, New York: Random House, 1994, pp. 108-113 and 440; Donald D. Hook, *Madmen of History*, New York: Dorset Press, 1976, pp. 45-60 and 165-177.

47. Con Coughlin, *Saddam: King of Terror*, New York: HarperCollins, 2002, p. xxvii.

48. Graham, Ibid., p. 7; italics in the original.

49. Terence T. Gorski, "The Role of Codependence in Relapse," Independence, MO: Herald House/Independence Press, 1991, audio-cassette series.

50. Milam and Ketcham, Ibid., pp. 64-65.

51. Study published by the Journal of the American Medical Association, May 3, 2000, "Characteristics of Child Passenger Deaths and Injuries Involving Drinking Drivers," Kyran P. Quinlan, MD, et al, 283: 2249-2252.

52. Reported in U.S. Department of Transportation, *DWI Detection and Standardized Field Sobriety Testing: Student Manual*, Oklahoma City, OK: National Highway Traffic Safety Administration, 1995, pp. V-5 to V-7.

53. LAPD Web Site, www.cityofla.org/LAPD/traffic/dre/drgdrvr.htm: Thomas E. Page, "The Drug Recognition Expert Response to the Drug Impaired Driver," pp. 5-6.

54. National Council on Alcoholism, reported by Robe, Ibid., p. 402.

55. D. Campbell and M. Graham, "Drugs and Alcohol in the Workplace: A Guide for Managers," New York: Facts on File Publications, 1988, p. 9.

56. STAND, Support Training Against Narcotic Dependency, Los Angeles Police Department handout, "Why STAND;" Thomas E. Backer, Ph.D., "Strategic Planning for Workplace Drug Abuse Programs," National

Institute on Drug Abuse, 1987, p. 4.

57. STAND, Ibid.

58. *"What makes a problem is a problem*....What causes trouble is trouble, and if your alcohol causes trouble, then alcohol is a problem for you." *"An alcoholic is somebody whose drinking causes serious life problems."* Father Martin, Ibid., pp. 35 and 34. Italics in the original.

59. Daniel Akst, *Wonder Boy – The Kid Who Swindled Wall Street,* New York: Charles Scribner's Sons, 1990, pp. 113, 270 and numerous other pages.

60. *Alcoholics Anonymous: The Story of How Many Thousands of Men and Women Have Recovered from Alcoholism,* New York: Alcoholics Anonymous World Services, Inc., Third Edition, 1976, p. 542.

61. Reported by Royce and Scratchley, Ibid., p. 117.

62. Donald Goodwin, MD, *Is Alcoholism Hereditary?,* New York: Ballantine Books, 1988, pp. 98-115.

63. Robe, Ibid., p. 172.

64. Everett R. Amundsen, *National Responsible Drivers* handbook, p. 26.

65. Robe, Ibid. p. 78.

66. New York, NY: Alcoholics Anonymous World Services, Inc., pamphlet: "20 Questions."

67. Thorburn, Ibid., pp. 64-80.

68. Graham, Ibid., p. 60, quoting Richard C. Bates, MD

69. Robe, Ibid., p. 267.

70. Stephen White, *Russia Goes Dry: Alcohol, State and Society,* Great Britain: Cambridge University Press, 1996, p. 43.

71. Dennis Wholey, Ed., *The Courage to Change: Personal Conversations About Alcoholism,* New York: Warner Books, 1984, p. 201.

72. Caroline Knapp, *Drinking: A Love Story,* New York: The Dial Press, 1996, p. 74.

73. "NCADD Fact Sheet: Alcohol and Other Drugs in the Workplace," National Council on Alcoholism and Drug Dependence, Inc., 12 West 221 Street, New York, NY 10010, reporting on National Institute on Drug Abuse, "Research on Drugs and the Workplace," NIDA Capsules, June, 1990, p. 1.

74. Ibid.; D. Campbell and M. Graham, Ibid.

75. Gorski and Miller, Ibid., p. 59

76. Milam and Ketcham, Ibid., p. 64

77. STAND, Ibid. Soviet research reported similar findings, suggesting the "efficiency" of the alcoholic worker was 36% less than that of non-drinkers. Reported in White, Ibid., p. 50.

78. Thorburn, Ibid., includes numerous stories of such victims, how addiction could have been identified in each case and actions that can be taken to prevent future tragedies even if already involved with the addict.

79. White, Ibid., p. 41.

80. The Los Angeles Times, "Where did we go wrong?" by Alex Kotlowitz, author of the 1991 book, *There Are No Children Here: The Story of Two Boys Growing Up in the Other America.* My copy of the article is undated.

81. Beth Polson and Newton Miller, Ph.D., *Not My Kid: a Parent's Guide to Kids and Drugs*, New York: Avon Books, 1984, pp. 79-97.

82. However, David Keirsey at www.keirsey.com suggests that ADHD is non-existent and, in reality, what appears to be ADHD is a result of having a mind that is interested in everything and which becomes easily bored. This is, of course, considered to be a character defect by some.

83. Milam and Ketcham, Ibid., p. 65.

84. D. Campbell and M. Graham, Ibid.

85. M. Bernstein, J.J. Mahoney, "Management Perspectives on Alcoholism: The Employer's Stake in Alcoholism Treatment," Occupational Medicine, Vol. 4, No. 2, 1989, pp. 223-232 and U.S. Department of Labor, "What Works: Workplaces Without Drugs," August, 1990, p. 3.

86. Richard Rovere, *Senator Joe McCarthy*, Methuen and Co., Ltd., 1960, quoted in Graham, Ibid., p. 21.

87. Robe, Ibid., p. 96.

88. The Role of Psychological Type and Temperament in diagnosing and treating addiction is discussed in Thorburn, Ibid., pp. 245-272 and 331-338, and in greater detail in Doug Thorburn, *Styles of Alcoholism: The Role of Type and Temperament in Diagnosing and Treating Addiction*, Northridge, CA: Galt Publishing, in publication 2005. This work is partly based on David Keirsey and Marilyn Bates, *Please Understand Me: Character & Temperament Types*, Del Mar, CA: Prometheus Nemesis Book Company, 1978, and Keirsey's student, Eve Delunas, *Survival Games Personalities Play*, Carmel, CA: SunInk Publications, 1992. *Styles of Alcoholism* links the Survival Games played by different Temperaments to specific Personality Disorders mimicked by addiction.

89. *Diagnostic and Statistical Manual of Mental Disorders*, Fourth Edition, Washington, DC: American Psychiatric Association, 1994.

90. *DSM-IV*, Ibid., pp. 649-650.

91. *The 16th Edition of the Merck Manual*, Whitehouse Station, NJ: Merck and Co., Inc., 1992, p. 1546.

92. Heston, Ibid.

93. Patty Duke and Kenneth Turan, *Call Me Anna: The Autobiography of Patty Duke*, New York: Bantam Books, 1987, pp. 90-91, 155, 169, 174, 196, 200-201, 203-205, 239 and 310.

94. Anne Wilson Schaef, "Recovering in an Addictive World," audio-tape,

10th Annual "Common Boundary" Conference, Boulder, CO: Sounds True Recordings, 1991.

95. Families of the Mentally Ill Collective, Nona Dearth, Chairman, *Families Helping Families Living With Schizophrenia*, New York: Avon Books, 1987, p. 7.

96. Henry Maudley, MD, *Responsibility in Mental Disease*, New York: D. Appleton and Company, 1897, pp. 305-306, citing D. Yellowlees, MD, "Insanity and Intemperance," *British Medical Journal*, October 4th, 1893. Maudley also noted in his discussion of what he termed "the indulgence" in liquor that "Short of the patent and undeniable ills which it is admitted on all hands to produce, it is at the bottom of manifold mischiefs that are never brought directly home to it." I am not the first to point out the fact that numerous behavioral problems that *should* be linked to alcoholism, are not.

97. *DSM-IV*, Ibid., p. 651.

98. *DSM-IV*, Ibid., p. 661.

99. Royce and Scratchley, Ibid., p. 132.

100. Cited in Robe, Ibid., pp. 383-384.

101. Nine out of 100,000 equals 90 out of one million. Since 10% of the population consists of alcoholics, there are about 100,000 alcoholics for every million people. The sum of 90 and 207, or all suicides, is 297. Dividing the alcoholic-suicides of 207 by the total number of suicides per one million population, 297, yields 70%.

102. Royce and Scratchley, Ibid., p. 178.

103. Milam and Ketcham, Ibid., p. 154.

104. Terence T. Gorski, *Understanding the Twelve Steps: A Guide for Counselors, Therapists, and Recovering People*, Independence, MO: Herald House/Independence Press, 1989, p. 23.

105. Saul Miller, with Jo Anne Miller, *Food for Thought: A New Look at Food and Behavior*, Englewood Cliffs, NJ: Prentice-Hall, 1979, p. 91, from a study by N. Rojas and A. F. Sanchi, "Archives of Legal Medicine," 11, 1941, p. 29, reported in *Natural Health, Sugar and the Criminal Mind*, by J. I. Rodale, New York: Pyramid Books, 1968.

106. D. Campbell and M. Graham, Ibid.

107. STAND, Ibid.

108. Toby Rice Drews, *The 350 Secondary Diseases/Disorders to Alcoholism*, South Plainfield, NJ: Bridge Publishing, 1985. James W. Smith, MD, Chief Medical Officer, Schick Chemical Dependency Programs, in a booklet entitled, "An Orientation on Alcoholism," no copyright date (probably written about 1982), p. 35, points out that the mortality rate from pneumonia is "far" higher in alcoholics than in the general population.

109. Milam and Ketcham, Ibid., pp. 90-91, citing Benjamin Kissin and

Maureen M. Kaley, "Alcohol and Cancer," in *The Biology of Alcoholism*, ed. Kissin and Begleiter, vol. 3, p. 481.

110. Ibid., p. 84.

111. Polson and Newton, Ibid., p. 52 and numerous other pages.

112. White, Ibid., p. 45. Considering our redefinition, most if not all of what is called "alcohol abuse" is probably early-stage alcoholism.

113. Royce and Scratchley, Ibid., p. 7.

114. Stephen Braun, *Buzz: The Science and Lore of Alcohol and Caffeine*, New York: Oxford University Press, 1996, pp. 52-59, has a terrific explanation of this.

115. Gitlow and Ford's comments reported in Robe, Ibid., pp. 157-158. The sedative-hypnotic drugs include barbiturates (Seconal, Nembutal), tranquilizers (Valium, Librium), Miltown, chloral hydrate and Quaaludes.

116. Graham, Ibid., p. 16.

117. Robe, Ibid., p. 160.

118. "Newsweek," October 30, 2000; reprinted in "Readers' Digest," in an article entitled, "Drunk Driver's Ed," May, 2001, pp. 70-72.

Bibliography

Alcoholics Anonymous: The Story of How Many Thousands of Men and Women Have Recovered from Alcoholism, New York: Alcoholics Anonymous World Services, Inc., Third Edition, 1976.

Akst, Daniel, *Wonder Boy – The Kid Who Swindled Wall Street*, New York: Charles Scribner's Sons, 1990.

Braun, Stephen, *Buzz: The Science and Lore of Alcohol and Caffeine*, New York: Oxford University Press, 1996.

Brubaker, Mike and Ken Estes, *Deadly Odds: Recovery From Compulsive Gambling*, New York: Simon and Schuster, Fireside/Parkside Books, 1994.

Carter, Dan, *The Politics of Rage*, New York: Simon & Schuster, 1995.

Coughlin, Con, *Saddam: King of Terror*, New York: HarperCollins, 2002.

Delunas, Eve, *Survival Games Personalities Play*, Carmel, CA: SunInk Publications, 1992.

Diagnostic and Statistical Manual of Mental Disorders, Fourth Edition, Washington, DC: American Psychiatric Association, 1994.

Drews, Toby Rice, *The 350 Secondary Diseases/Disorders to Alcoholism*, South Plainfield, NJ: Bridge Publishing, 1985.

Duke, Patty and Kenneth Turan, *Call Me Anna: The Autobiography of Patty Duke*, New York: Bantam Books, 1987.

Dunn, Donald H., *Ponzi! The Boston Swindler*, New York: McGraw-Hill Book Company, 1975.

Eberle, Paul and Shirley, *The Abuse of Innocence: The McMartin Preschool Trial*, Buffalo, New York: Prometheus Books, 1993.

Families of the Mentally Ill Collective, Nona Dearth, Chairman, *Families Helping Families Living With Schizophrenia*, New York: Avon Books, 1987.

Frady, Marshall, *Wallace*, New York: Random House, 1996.

Goodwin, Donald W., MD, *Alcoholism and the Writer*, Kansas City: Andrews and McMeel, 1988.

Goodwin, Donald W., MD, *Is Alcoholism Hereditary?* New York: Ballantine Books, 1988.

Gorski, Terence T., "The Role of Codependence in Relapse," Independence, MO: Herald House/Independence Press, 1991, audio-cassette series.

Gorski, Terence T. and Merlene Miller, *Staying Sober: A Guide for Relapse Prevention*, Independence, MO: Herald House/Independence Press.

Gorski, Terence T., *Understanding the Twelve Steps: A Guide for Counselors, Therapists, and Recovering People,*

Independence, MO: Herald House/Independence Press, 1989.

Graham, James, *The Secret History of Alcoholism: The Story of Famous Alcoholics and Their Destructive Behavior*, Rockport, MA: Element Books, 1996.

Grinspooon, Lester, MD, and James B. Bakalar, JD, "Mental Health Review," President and Fellows of Harvard College, 1990.

Hayakawa, S.I. *Language in Thought and Action*, Harcourt, Brace and Company: New York, 1949.

Heston, Leonard L., MD and Renate Heston, R.N., *The Medical Casebook of Adolf Hitler*, New York: Stein and Day, 1980.

Hook, Donald D., *Madmen of History*, New York: Dorset Press, 1976.

Hyman, B. D., *My Mother's Keeper: A daughter's candid portrait of her famous mother*, New York: William Morrow and Co., 1985.

Johnson, Vernon, *I'll Quit Tomorrow*, San Francisco, CA: Harper and Row, 1980.

Keirsey, David and Marilyn Bates, *Please Understand Me: Character & Temperament Types*, Del Mar, CA: Prometheus Nemesis Book Company, 1978.

Knapp, Caroline, *Drinking: A Love Story*, New York: The Dial Press, 1996.

Martin, Father Joseph C., *Chalk Talks on Alcohol*, San Francisco, CA: Harper and Row, 1989.

Maudley, Henry, MD, *Responsibility in Mental Disease*, New York: D. Appleton and Company, 1897.

Milam, Dr. James R. and Katherine Ketcham, *Under the Influence: A Guide to the Myths and Realities of Alcoholism*, New York: Bantam Books, 1983.

Miller, Saul, with Jo Anne Miller, *Food for Thought: A New Look at Food and Behavior*, Englewood Cliffs, NJ: Prentice-Hall, 1979.

Morrison, Martha, *White Rabbit: A Doctor's Story of Her Addiction and Recovery*, New York: Crown Publishers, 1989.

National Council on Alcoholism and Drug Dependence, Inc., "Fact Sheet: Alcoholism and Alcohol Related Problems," 12 West 21 Street, New York, NY 10010, May, 1995.

Polson, Beth and Newton Miller, Ph.D., *Not My Kid: a Parent's Guide to Kids and Drugs*, New York: Avon Books, 1984.

Robe, Lucy Barry, *Co-Starring Famous Women and Alcohol: the dramatic truth behind the tragedies and triumphs of 200 celebrities*, Minneapolis, MN: CompCare Publications, 1986.

Roy, Maria, Ed., *Battered Women: A Psychosociological Study of Domestic Violence*, New York: Van Nostrand, 1977.

Royce, James E. and David Scratchley, *Alcoholism and Other Drug Problems*, New York: The Free Press, 1996.

Schaef, Anne Wilson, "Recovering in an Addictive World," audio-tape, 10th Annual "Common Boundary" Conference,

Boulder, CO: Sounds True Recordings, 1991.

Thorburn, Doug, *Drunks, Drugs & Debits: How to Recognize Addicts and Avoid Financial Abuse*, Northridge, CA: Galt Publishing, 2000.

Thorburn, Doug, *Get Out of the Way! How to Identify and Avoid a Driver Under the Influence*, Northridge, CA: Galt Publishing, 2002.

Thorburn, Doug, *Styles of Alcoholism: The Role of Type and Temperament in Diagnosing and Treating Addiction*, Northridge, CA: Galt Publishing, in publication 2005.

Tiebout, Harry M., MD, "The Ego Factors in Surrender to Alcoholism," New Brunswick, NJ: Journal of Studies on Alcohol, Inc., Vol. 15.

U.S. Department of Transportation, *DWI Detection and Standardized Field Sobriety Testing: Student Manual*, Oklahoma City, OK: National Highway Traffic Safety Administration, 1995.

Vaillant, George E., *The Natural History of Alcoholism Revisited*, Cambridge, MA: Harvard University Press, 1995.

White, Stephen, *Russia Goes Dry: Alcohol, State and Society*, Great Britain: Cambridge University Press, 1996.

Wholey, Dennis, Ed., *The Courage to Change: Personal Conversations About Alcoholism*, New York: Warner Books, 1984.

Zhisui, Dr. Li , *The Private Life of Chairman Mao*, New York: Random House, 1994.

Index

16, 90
National Highway Traffic Safety Administration, 64-67, 89, 92
Neocortex, 19, 41, 51, 101, 104
Neurotransmitters, 17-18, 26, 85, 118-119
NHTSA (see National Highway Traffic Safety Administration)
Non-addicts (see non-alcoholics)
Non-alcoholics, 1, 18-19, 35, 37, 50, 60, 63, 67, 71, 81-82, 112-113, 117, 124
Nystagmus, Horizontal Gaze, 70

O
Obsessive-Compulsive Personality Disorder, 101
Occupational choice and alcoholism, 37, 39
Opiates, 115, 119
Other-destructive behaviors, 31-73
Overachievement (see achievement, over)
Overpermissiveness as a clue to alcoholism, 93
Overspending as a clue to alcoholism (see spending, over)
Oxycontin, 115

P
Pacino, Al, 36
Pain as the addict's best friend, 13, 53, 124
Pancreatic problems due to alcoholism, 111, 113-114
Paranoia, 47, 62
Paranoid-Schizophrenic, 14
Paraphernalia, 112-113
Parole, 126
Partying as a clue to alcoholism, 54, 78, 118
Paul, Henri, 40, 82, 115
Percodan, 102

About the Author

Doug Thorburn is one of the world's foremost experts in identifying alcoholism based on behavior patterns. He has spoken to and provided continuing education for professional organizations, including the California Association for Alcohol and Drug Educators (CAADE), the California Association of Alcohol and Drug Abuse Counselors (CAADAC), and the California Association of Drinking Driver Treatment Programs (CADDTP).

In addition, Doug has authored two books prior to *How to Spot Hidden Alcoholics: Using Behavioral Clues to Recognize Addiction in its Early Stages* — *Drunks, Drugs & Debits: How to Recognize Addicts and Avoid Financial Abuse* (2000) and *Get Out of the Way! How to Identify and Avoid a Driver Under the Influence* (2002). He is currently writing two others — *Myths and Realities of Alcoholism* (in publication late 2004) and *Styles of Alcoholism: Using Psychological Type and Personality Disorders to Identify and Treat Addiction* (in publication 2005).

Doug is also the president and founder of the PrevenTragedy Foundation, a non-profit organization dedicated to educating the public on the importance of early identification of alcoholism and how to identify this disease *before* tragedy strikes.

Other Books by Doug Thorburn

Drunks, Drugs & Debits

One of the most comprehensive books on addiction ever written, *Drunks, Drugs & Debits* proposes a paradigm shift in the way we view and treat alcohol and other drug addiction. Basic enough to be understood by laypersons and detailed enough to interest the professionals, *Drunks, Drugs & Debits* leaves no aspect of alcoholism unexplored.

"Exciting and insightful...One of the most important books ever written...a landmark treatise."

> Dr. Forest Tennant, Dr. P.H., author,
> *The Legal Identification of Drug Use*

"I highly recommend this unique, eye-opening book."

> Katherine Ketcham, author,
> *Beyond the Influence and Under the Influence*

"An entirely fresh look...Outstanding!"

> Audrey DeLaMarte, bookreviewer for
> "The Phoenix" and "Steps to Recovery"

"A unique contribution....'must' reading."

> "Midwest Book Review" and "Internet Bookwatch,"

"Contains vital information that everyone should know."
Terence T. Gorski, author,
Sober: and Staying That Way

"Extraordinary and unique...allows the reader to view situations from an entirely new perspective. The field of addiction needs this book."
G. Douglas Talbott, MD, FASAM, FACP, Past-President,
American Society of Addiction Medicine

"*Drunks, Drugs & Debits* is incredible. Thorburn provides some powerful tools to help you detect addicts around you and avoid the havoc they wreak.
Randy Cassingham, ThisIsTrue.com and
HeroicStories.com

"Told with passion and backed with facts, *Drunks, Drugs & Debits* is a compelling look into the relationships among addiction, financial management and personality."
Alice M. and Lisa L. Fairhurst, authors,
Effective Teaching, Effective Learning:
Making the Personality Connection in Your classroom

"*Drunks, Drugs & Debits* should lead to a revolution in several applied sciences, including psychiatry, psychology, criminology and medicine. Everyone should read this book, as addiction affects all of us whether we know it or not."
Robert Prechter, author, *Elliott Wave Theory* and
Socionomics: The Science of History and Social Prediction

Get Out of the Way!

Get Out of the Way! is a concise and easy-to-read introduction to alcoholism, particularly in its hidden early stages. It is written to assist both lay persons and law enforcers in identifying those drivers who may be lethal to the rest of us.

"Doug's methods of identification improve the odds of detection and intervention. I commend him for his enlightened and practical insights into the mind and behaviors of the impaired driver."

Sergeant Thomas Page,
Drug Recognition Expert, Sergeant, LAPD, ret.

"Police officers, policy makers and citizens alike will find this book innovative, enlightening and stimulating."
Donald Boon, LAPD officer

"As an interventionist with more than 13 years in the field, I thank Doug Thorburn for his insight and state-of-the-art concepts."

Pat Moomey, C.A.T.S.

"Doug's books are essential for anyone struggling to make sense of the destructive or bizarre behaviors found in others."

Claudia Black, author, *It Will Never Happen to Me*

Order Form

Fax Orders: 818.363.3111　　　　　*Phone Orders: 800.482.9424*
www.PrevenTragedy.com
Galt Publishing; P.O. Box 7777; Northridge, CA 91327

_____ *copies of "Drunks, Drugs & Debits" @ $29.95 each*　　$_____

_____ *copies of "Get Out of the Way!" @ $12.95 each*　　　$_____

_____ *copies of "How to Spot Hidden Alcoholics" @ $14.95*　$_____

Sales Tax: 8.25% for California residents　　　　　　　$_____
We pay shipping
　　　　　　　　　　　　Total Investment　　　$_____

I wish to pay by:
　　_____ *Check (enclosed)*
　　_____ *Visa* _____ *Mastercard*　　　_____ *Discover*
　　Card Number: _____ _____ _____ _____ *Exp.* ___/___
　　Name on Card: _____
　　Signature (required): _____

Deliver to: Name _____
　　　　　　Address _____
　　　　　　City _____ *State* _____ *Zip Code* _____

Telephone Number : _____
E-mail Address (for updates): _____

Please send additional information on:
　　　　_____ *Other books and tapes by Doug Thorburn*
　　　　_____ *Quantity prices on books*
　　　　_____ *Speaking & Seminars*